A New Age of God

One Life...One Love...Eternal

Judy Bell

Copyright © 2012 Judy Bell
All rights reserved.

ISBN 10: 0615621910
ISBN 13: 9780615621913

INTRODUCTION

One God not one religion... Seeking the Lord in all things

John 14:23. *If a man loves me, he will keep my words: and my Father will love him, and we will come unto him, and make our abode with him. John 14:26, But the Comforter, which is the Holy Ghost, whom the Father will send in my name, He shall teach you all things, and bring all things into remembrance, whatsoever I have said unto you.*

Society today lives through the mind, the flesh and the emotions, constantly striving to feel alive and it is not satisfying them. This is what the bible calls carnal living. Doctors are trying to solve the problem through the prescription pad and it only makes the problem worse. People are trying to solve the problem with sex, drugs and alcohol. Depression and dissatisfaction are growing more and more daily and it is time to consider a new way of living.

Everyone is running faster and faster trying to achieve something they can't catch because it cannot be bought. We have all been sold a bill of goods by the media whose job it is to sell us more and more useless stuff. We are being reprogrammed into acceptance of things as they appear through the influence of movies, television, the internet etc. Everyone wants you to accept that this is all there is and you are at the mercy of the world for your

A New Age of God

existence. This is the greatest seed of deceit and it is designed to keep you powerless.

> **Psalm 102:13.** *But you shall arise, and have mercy upon Zion (believers): for the time to favor her, yes the set time, is come.*

God has a set time for all things and something wonderful is starting to happen; People are beginning to wake up out of their hypnotized sleep and are starting to acknowledge the dissatisfaction and the hunger they feel is coming from emptiness within. The love of God is reaching out to the people in an attempt touch those of His children who are seeking the truth. Some have tried religion to attempt to find God but the church failed to touch their hearts and they feel even more lost and cannot figure out what happened to God. If you love Jesus but hate religion don't despair. Jesus came to give you the secret to life not a religion.

I love talking to young people to try to understand what they are going through and how they think. Teenagers and young people in their twenties tell me they really love Jesus but they hate the church. They think it is all dogma and the church is full of hypocrites and they cannot relate to any of it or they feel judged and dismissed as unworthy. No one wants to listen to them and they feel isolated and misunderstood. They feel something is wrong with religion but they don't know what it is but it just doesn't feel right. They need to understand they are Devine by birth from the Father and they can hold the keys to the kingdom. The power that is their birthright is there waiting for them to claim.

We must get past appearances and listen to what's going on in their lives. They feel pressured by society and their

A New Age of God

peers and they feel alone. Most have been abused or neglected and they are confused and angry. Only a small percentage has had any type of mentoring on how to live. Their only guide is the media and the movies. How can they show respect if they are not respected?

Most of all they do not feel loved and accepted in the world and have no expectations for their future. We all receive what we expect so how do we change their expectations and therefore change lives and attitudes. Everyone wants to be loved and accepted whether they want to admit it or not.

Millions of people old and young are seeking a new path; a new way to live that provides satisfaction and peace. I want you to find the happiness that comes from the loving relationship that your heart has been craving.

First of all I want to introduce you to a stranger in most of the world today, the Holy Spirit. The Holy Spirit is the Comforter and the guiding voice of God and He has been virtually eliminated from the current church and been relegated to something that is talked about in the bible but does not apply to the modern world. These are the people, who tell us the same things about miracles. They are not intentionally misleading the people it is just that they have never been taught that the Holy Spirit is a living presence that can be felt and heard and to allow the Holy Spirit to guide them.

Many people have felt the touch of the Comforter in times of heartbreak and crisis. They speak of a peace that engulfed them and helped them to survive when they felt their life was over or irreparable. Usually this is when they are in deep prayer reaching out to God. They are so lost and so hurt that they finally give complete focus on God and He reaches out to them and comforts their troubled souls.

A New Age of God

Pastors often talk about when the anointing falls as they are leading their congregations in worship and suddenly the anointing of the Holy Spirit falls and they are inspired to change their message. The Holy Spirit steps in and the presence of God guides the church service and people's lives and hearts are changed. These are sacred events of the Holy Spirit working within their ministry and these events need to be witnessed and praised. The more praise and gratitude the more God will reach out to the assembly. When people truly assemble and seek the face of God the results are miraculous.

The current church is trying to draw in the people with a show, entertainment with big bands, and huge monitors. It might get them through the door but they don't realize they aren't really looking for a show, what they are looking for is a touch of God. The spiritual food you receive when you are touched by God is the purpose of worship, but society has programmed everyone to expect to be entertained in everything they do and the presence of God is not considered or expected. It is easy to get revved up in the music and the moment but what happens after you go home? Does life just come off pause and it becomes business as usual? Is God left at the door to the church or does He come home with you?

God will not come second to anything! Church is for honoring and worshipping God and it is a privilege to go and show my Father my love for Him. You cannot leave God at the door and not take Him with you. If you would decide to keep God in your heart and put everything aside for a little while each day for God it would change your whole world.

We live in an era of instant gratification without involvement or commitment. Your expectation cannot be just getting a feel good moment and move on back to

A New Age of God

your same old life. Why not take the time to open up your heart and let the Holy Spirit rock your world.

God is not a spectator sport; He wants your undivided devotion. So many people go to church with the wrong attitude not really looking for God and leave feeling empty and they use their attitude to become a self-fulfilling prophecy that reinforces their belief that church isn't for them and God just doesn't speak to them. Church might be nice but it isn't an essential part of their life.

Church is not a duty it is an opportunity that should be honored. You do not go to church for your entertainment, you go to give praise to the Father, give Him glory and gratitude to the Lord. This is your opportunity to show up and show out for the God who is always there for you. It is your chance to unite with fellow worshippers and publicly honor your Lord and Savior that gave everything to bring us to the Father. We should rejoice in prayer, song and word. If we show up, act out in praise and seek Him, the Holy Spirit will make His presence known and that is when you really get entertained!

> **John 13: 32.** *If God be glorified in him, God shall also glorify him in himself, and shall straightaway glorify him.*

There is a cloud of deceit that is surrounding the planet much like a thick fog bank. The darkness is shrouding the eyes of the people and the enemy is attempting to shroud the people from the light of God. This fog blankets our minds and consists of the lies that have been implanted in the church itself almost 1,950 years ago, the lie of society that says we have evolved past needing God and the deception of our egos that is keeping us self-centered, that binds us to earthly things.

A New Age of God

These are some of the lies that keep us bound in darkness:
The world around you is all there is and we have no control.
We do not need the guidance of an unseen and unproven God.
Jesus was a great teacher with great ideas but was not Devine.
We can never reconcile with other races, cultures or religions.
The way it is, is the way it always be.
You cannot change the nature of man.

My question to you is why not? Why can't we reconcile with others? Why can't we change the way it has always been? If we start to look with a new understanding then we will recognize the lies in our lives and they will lose their power to influence the way we see the world and recognize the truth. Why condemn a whole group of people because of a few that who claim to represent the whole group?

We have judged the religious community because of ministers and organizations that have publicly condemned the rest of the world because it isn't exactly the way they see the world and how they worship God. They are bogged down in manmade laws and want to tell you how to dress; how to think and how to worship.

We as a species have a tendency to condemn whole cultures for their difference and the acts of a minority of the people, just as we have allowed a few radicals to paralyze us with fear and condemnation because a sect of a religion has committed insane acts against those who are different. The religious leaders have poisoned their minds against other religions and have created a culture of hate.

Gangs around the world have terrorized and taken control of whole communities because we have allowed them to stigmatize their race be it Hispanic, Asian, African American or White Supremacists etc. They want us to condemn them, throw our hands up, give up on them and walk away so they may have free realm on their community.

These are the lies of Satan that have become generational curses to keep us separated and at each other's throats. We cannot afford to be divided kept living as animals fighting against each other in pacts. Look at what a generational curse did to Czechoslovakia. A blood feud causes a war to rage and virtually destroys that beautiful country. Thousands of people died for nothing! The blood feud continues on for another generation.

The greatest gift is to love and be loved. One love...One life....One spirit eternal

The secret to the universe is love. We are loved above all others as the chosen of the universe by the Creator. We may all be separate entities but we are all of the one spirit which is the Creator. God gave us the ultimate gift; He created us in His image, endowed us with His gifts and chooses to love us above all others intending for us to walk in spiritual awareness. It is time for us to step up and take ownership of our inheritance.

God wants us to worship the One God not a religion that man has built with their logical mind. The church came under organized control since AD 314 when The Emperor Constantine set himself up as the head of the church and decided what was worthy of being included in the bible. Constantine was a pagan who primarily worshipped the Sun God when he decided to convert to Christianity even though he continued to worship the Sun God.

A New Age of God

His public agenda was to amend the divisions that were rife in the church and reconstruct the teachings so that the common mind could relate to the church, but in reality he wanted to take the teachings of Jesus and integrate his pagan beliefs into Christianity. They said what they wanted was a church that would not confuse the average man so they could bring the pagans to Christ and wound up altering the message and purpose that Jesus came to teach and died to give us. They took their pagan beliefs, combined with the logic of the mind and inserted it into the church and altered the working relationship of God with His children.

This was an abomination to the Lord and an uncounted millions have been led to worship false idols and to accept the teaching of intersession from manmade saints to find grace and find salvation. The bible states you must pray to the Father of us all in the name of Jesus Christ. Nowhere in the bible does it say to pray to a manmade saint for intersession with the Lord. We all have guides, guardians and teachers to try to help you grow and learn but we do not pray to them. That would be worshipping them for doing their assigned work. God is tired of His people being led in the name of God down a pagan path.

> **John 5:22-23** *For the Father judges no man, but has committed all judgment to the Son: that all should honor the Son, even as they honor the Father. He that honors not the Son honors not the Father which has sent Him.*

No man can be Christ on the earth; Jesus sits at the right hand of God on the judgment throne and only through Jesus can you receive salvation. Worship no one but God and you will honor the Creator. Pray to the Father in the name of Jesus and no other.

A New Age of God

Do not allow the folly of mankind to become an excuse not to believe the bible is the word of God. There is a whole different meaning within the word of God. God has kept His meaning and His message hidden within the bible and the key to understanding is through the interpretation of the Holy Spirit. You can read the bible through every year and not glean the intentions and meanings of God until you start to study the word after receiving the Holy Spirit. Revelations and understanding await you within the word.

The bible is the study manual for your life and not just a book for casual reading. God gave us the Old Testament to give us the law and to show how mankind was not able to stand in his own righteousness and to provide the prophecy to ready us to accept the Messiah. The New Testament gave us the keys to salvation and how to accept the righteousness of Christ as our own. The bible holds the word of God and with the touch of our supernatural God it will bring His intentions to you and make the meaning your revelation.

> **John 15:3.** *Now you are clean through the word which I have spoken to you.*

Our God is a nondenominational Creator and is sick of the arbitrary rules and regulations that limit the worship and relationship of His children. A supernatural God cannot be understood by logic. The spirit of man and his logical mind are too entirely different things. God does not care what you wear, how you groom your body or how long your hair is; what he does care about is the condition of your heart and your faith. Faith is operating in the Word.

A New Age of God

We need church but not so we can follow the dogma of men or see what someone is wearing or what car they bought but to seek fellowship in Christ of those with like precious mind and faith. When people of faith gather together it allows the Lord so show up and show out. Church is fellowship with teaching of the word and guidance with purpose to allow seekers the opportunity for God to touch their hearts.

When we worship in united fellowship seeking the Holy Spirit, then God will step out and His presence will be unmistakable. Miracles will start to occur and become the expectation (you must expect to receive). If this is what you want to achieve in your church the key is to allow the Holy Spirit the opportunity and freedom to lead the worship. God wants you to praise and worship Him in any manner you want regardless of you heritage or background. Jesus Christ who is the son of God was born and walked the Earth to bring a way out of the madness and to offer us salvation. This is the Jesus Way.

> **John 4:48.** *Except you see signs and wonders, you will not believe.*

Jesus wants everyone to find their way to His presence and this book is written to help people start to find their way back to the essence of their faith. Jesus came to provide the teachings and guidance to allow man to come to the Father on a personal basis and to eliminate the need for the Priests to be the contact with God. I welcome you to walk with me for a short while, discern the truth for yourself and see if we can get to a closer walk with the Creator.

When God calls you, you are not too old or too young. You do not have too much to do and you cannot blame your finances for not answering the call. I don't care what you have done in the past or who you are today. God can clean up your life and heal your heart; you will have a new life through Jesus Christ our Lord and Savior.

> **John 15:7.** *If you abide in me, and my words abide in you, you shall ask what you will, and it shall be done unto you.*

Who you think you are without Christ is an illusion created by the Deceiver to keep you from coming awake and seeing your purpose. God calls His children, He forgives the past and He remakes us into what you are meant to be. The time has come to get to God's level in talking thinking and action. Take possession of your inheritance for you are of royal lineage and you are meant to be either a priest or a king in His Kingdom.

This life is the gift of God for us to possess and if we refuse we are dishonoring God and limiting our life. There is a way to own your own power within to do the works of God and to change this demon world back into Gods paradise.

The world needs people who have a vision of what God intends life on Earth to be. If you love Jesus but not the current church I may be able to help you understand why you feel that way. You need to consider walking the Jesus Way and see what a spiritual life has to offer. It is not enough to say Jesus loved us all so we do not have to worry about salvation because God set forth the guidelines for living and He expects each of us to follow the laws of His kingdom. We must rise above the animals and return to a purer spiritual state, receive salvation and find a unity of spirit.

A New Age of God

Jesus was a living example of what the true essence and abilities of the spiritual man should be and Jesus died to prove there is a living God that transcends death and to allow you to live in grace in direct relationship with the Father through the Holy Spirit. Once we receive the Holy Spirit and we start to have fellowship with like-minded people then we can start to bring the non-believers with us to church and God will provide the miracles.

If we step up, God will step out because one miracle is worth a 100,000 sermons. God will show the people who are worshiping a God of vengeance and hate will touch their heart and they will come to see what life with a living, loving and forgiving God can mean to their lives. Living the Jesus Way can eliminate the hate and strife that exists between the tribes of man.

Jesus can heal the scars of the past that have kept different races and cultures apart. Those of us that have suffered from discrimination and hate or generational seeds of deceit will find healing and we can bond in unity as it was intended for all mankind. We should see our differences is a gift that should be celebrated. We all bring different gifts and perspectives to the table and should be shared and enjoyed. The differences of our skin is superficial that allowed us to live in the climate of our forefathers.

The First Nations can bring us a closer bond with the earth and a new approach to the living within the spirit. People can no longer be judged from the European view but be accepted and honored for their culture. Regardless of what continent you are from Jesus wants you to get to know Him and through the Holy Spirit live a life of honor and dignity. All God asks is that you worship Him and do not merge any other beliefs within the worship of Him.

Through the grace of God we can reconcile the past and become brothers in Christ. This is a process that brings us into unity with God and anyone can grow in faith and achieve the relationship that has been lacking in their lives.

Most Christian churches take you as far as salvation and just leave you there like you have gone as far as you need in Christ. The revelations of the Holy Spirit have been hidden from man and it is time for it to become available to all who want to have a closer walk with the Father. That is the pivotal point in a person's life but it is not the omega; it is the alpha of a beautiful journey.

When faith is truly engaged, you don't hold it; it holds you and makes you whole. You can live without fear but to succeed you must take possession of your faith. When you own something you do not doubt it is yours or what it will or won't do; the same is true of faith, because it is absolute! Faith resides in the word of God. We all have moments of doubt and fear but the secret is to put it aside and pray in faith and knowing. This is allowing God to take over and resolve the problem.

This is your inheritance and it is time to receive; God wants you to be successful and to live in affluence. It is time to stop believing you must live in poverty or believing the lie that you must sacrifice your life to be a person of God.

Why not give it a try? If you get one nugget of truth out of this then it is worth your time and energy. Worship and relationship is not complicated, all you need is an open mind and an open heart. Lead with your heart not your logical mind and listen carefully to what your heart tells you it will lead you to the truth.

CHAPTER 1

The Awakening

Ephesians 5:14. *Awake you that sleep, and arise from the dead and Christ shall give you light.*

There is a new age of God awakening around the planet. It has been prophesied that the year 2012 is the end of the world by the Mayans and the Hopi Indians, but this is not the end of times; it is the beginning of a new awareness and attitude that will include a new openness to matters of faith. People will be given the ability to see the truth with new eyes and understanding. Many problems that were insurmountable will suddenly be solved with a change of attitudes and solutions to long standing problems will seem obvious.

We will see what has been holding us back both spiritually and within society. The change in the attitude of the world will chance the dynamic of man's perception of the problems we face. For if two or more gather together of like mind the Lord will hear the petition and an answer will surface within the group.

A New Age of God

When you face a project pray for direction, ask for solutions to allow the job to be performed and begin to gather your team. The Lord will provide the answers and direction you should take. This is making God a partner in your work.

We are at a crossroads on the entire planet and if we don't choose to change we will continue on this downward spiral into absolute darkness. If we go on living in the same old way we will destroy our planet in the name of progress and we will continue living in a world where it will not be safe to walk the streets or raise our children.

The same people in the media that talk about social injustice can't see to decide what they want. One minute they are yelling like Chicken Little that the sky is falling and society is imploding and the next minute they rail against God and tell us that God is only superstition, which divides us and religion is something that is not needed in this modern society.

A small percentage of self-righteous preachers have the media spot light, which focuses on their ultra conservative views which condemn the whole world if it does not agree with their viewpoint. The enemy uses their self-righteousness to condemn the whole Christian faith. There is room for all faiths and when one member of the faith tries to speak for everyone then no one listens and we all become condemned.

The enemy is using every tool he has to stop the revival of God awareness and keep the world in darkness. Satan is attacking those that are working to bring forth an awareness of the will of God in a futile attempt to make us shut up and go away. My God's truth is stronger than anything the spreader of deceit and doubt can come up with. God is calling the lost, the confused and the seekers and He will not stop regardless of what the media, the government or even what you and I do.

A New Age of God

> **Revelation 12:7-9.** *And there was a war in Heaven: Michael and his angels fought against the dragon; and the dragon fought and his angels, and prevailed not; neither was their place found any more in Heaven. And the great dragon (Lucifer) was cast out, that old serpent, called the Devil, and Satan, which deceives the whole world: he was cast into the earth, and his angels were cast out with him.*

> **Ephesians 6:12.** *For we wrestle not against flesh and blood, but against principalities, against powers, against the rulers of darkness of this world, against spiritual wickedness in high places.*

More and more people have the urge to find a closer relationship with God and the urging will continue to get stronger and stronger until the ones who are being called decide to sit down, quiet their minds and listen to what He is saying to them. You have more love awaiting you than you can imagine. He wants you to act and walk in faith; to live an intended life.

Every one of us has a purpose and all you need to do is to open your eyes and your heart to find your destined life.

> **John 3:17.** *For God sent NOT His Son into the world to condemn the world; but that the world through Him might be saved.*

Jesus wants each of us to realize our worth and he has the power to bring forgiveness to each of us. Deep within each of us abides a deep inborn knowledge that we have one life (eternal), one love (eternal) and one spirit (eternal).

A New Age of God

God planted that knowledge within so we could have an inner compass to find our way to Him.

Unfortunately we are a bipolar species; the logical mind analyses everything and wants a logical explanation and we have the spiritual self that operates from the guidance of the Holy Spirit whose purpose is to guide us on our true path. The logical mind cannot fathom the ways and works of God. You cannot get to God through the mind, the path lies in the spirit through the heart.

To awaken the spirit within we need to understand what we are dealing with and approach understanding with an open heart. We need to understand where we came from and how we got to where we are and how we can change to what we need to be.

If we are to learn to change how we see ourselves then we must understand who we are and how we got where we are today. Man was meant to be a spiritual being and animals were meant to be separate entities; we were not intended to live and act as animals who survive on instinct and urges. We are not a product of evolution; we were created by God in His image to be His representative on earth; to have dominion and to be the care takers of paradise.

> **Genesis 2:16-17.** *And God commanded the man, saying, of every tree of the garden you may freely eat: But of the tree of the knowledge of good and evil, thou shall not eat of it: for it the day that you eat thereof you will surely die.*

> **Romans 8:6.** *For to be carnally (emotionally) minded is death; but to be spiritually minded is life and peace.*

A New Age of God

The original garden was a paradise where all things were provided for. Man was created by God in His image to be loved above all the other creations and man lived in a pure spiritual state. Man was able to live as of a man in the garden or he could exist in the spiritual realm where he walked with God whenever God beckoned him.

The essence of man in the original state as was as designed by the creator for man to coexist as spirit and man, but God gave man the free will to choose as he pleased but there were laws and prohibitions he needed to follow. God wanted man to choose a life of obedience and be blessed in life and spirit. That is the definition of the life God was speaking of.

In paradise stood two trees, one intended for man (the tree of life) that provided all man needed to sustain him and one that contained all the knowledge of good and evil including all the urges and instincts for the animals (this tree held all the knowledge the animals needed to survive; carnal desires were provided for the animals to propagate the species).

Enter the being that was called the serpent. He was jealous of the loving relationship man had with the creator and all the abilities and blessings that man had been given. The serpent knew that he would never possess the things and abilities of man. He was jealous because he could not walk as an equal with God, so he plotted to bring man down and separate man from his creator. He decided to convince Eve that it was a jealous and selfish God that wanted to deprive them from the knowledge held within the fruit. The lie was that the fruit held the knowledge of God and if they wanted to be Gods themselves all they had to do was eat of the fruit.

This downfall of man was the original seed of deceit and this was the original sin of mankind and

A New Age of God

has been passed down growing stronger with each generation.

When Eve listened to the serpent, he spoke to her ego and she craved more and wanted to be as God not just walk with Him so she ate the fruit of carnal knowledge and instantly became infected with the instincts and emotions that were meant for the animal kingdom. She was flooded with lust and deceit and started to see things with new feelings and desire. She was overcome with these carnal feelings and used them to seduce Adam into joining her. In an instant their being changed from being focused on God and walking in spirit and became grounded with the desires of the Earth.

There was no shame in their nakedness (innocence) before their infection; there was innocence in their wholeness as they walked through the garden with God. They had their pure essence of body, mind and spirit that they were created with. The minute they ate the forbidden fruit they were contaminated with all the instincts of the animals; man was attracted to all the evil that flooded his mind and this acted much like a virus spreading throughout their consciousness.

> **Genesis 6:5.** *And God saw that the wickedness of mans was great in the earth, and that every imagination of the thoughts of his heart was only evil continually.*

Their pure essence was destroyed and they realized their shame which has now separated them from God. They tried to hide so God would not see their shame of the knowledge that had flooded their soul and convicted them in their disobedience. They could not repent, they could not go back and mankind was changed from a spiritually

A New Age of God

focused being to living at the mercy of his conscious mind for survival.

The veil of separation fell between man and God. Mankind would never be able to see the world the same way again. Man was attracted to all things evil in the mind and the spirit of the carnal impulses blinded their Godly spiritual eyes and they began to see and think with the mind of the animals and their minds teemed with the knowledge of the evils that were possible. They knew lust, jealousy, hate and deceit for the first time and there was no going back.

Every human being has been infected through the generations with this carnal infection and all the urges that go with the territory of the animal kingdom. Instead of tending to the earth we are consumed with a blood lust that seems to grow with each generation.

There is a cure for this infection but for this to manifest a person had to be born without the infection of the animals. To walk and show the true path of a man led by the Father he had to be born pure without deceit. That is why God took the Word and wrapped it in flesh. The Word became flesh and bone, conceived by the Holy Spirit and implanted in Mary who was a virgin and His holy name is Jesus.

This had to occur so He would not be contaminated with the virus of man and could be born with the pure essence of the Father. The blood of the Father circulated in His veins to protect Him so that He could walk among us in the purity to show us all the spirituality and faith we all were intended to have. He came here to show us how to overcome the animal within, to recognize the deceit of the enemy and awaken the essence of God which lies within. Jesus brought us the quiet voice of the Comforter, the Holy Spirit.

A New Age of God

Satan wants us to listen to the roaring of the animal that rages within manipulating the ego, the emotions and the logical mind. If we quiet the beast and carefully listen we will hear the whisper of the Comforter that is waiting to be the voice you choose to listen to. The Holy Spirit is the voice that wants to guide you to higher and higher levels of the Father.

The Deceiver is the voice in the world that rationalizes your actions and tells you everyone does it; no harm no foul; everything you do is ok because life on Earth is survival of the fittest. He calls you to look at the world and give witness to what you see with the eyes of man.

Satan is the voice that convinces you that if God didn't want you to do that why did He make that temptation in the first place? He doesn't mention that it wouldn't be a temptation if we hadn't already fallen we wouldn't be dominated by the animal within.

God's original intention was for mankind to be a treasured child and be able to walk at His side. God created us to live in a certain manner that has now been lost to the world and we can only imagine what a magnificent life that would have been.

This carnal side of man smothers the spiritual side of most people and they live like animals instead of the men they are supposed to be. They feel so dead and lost they try supplementing the dark void within with drugs, sex or alcohol. That is why they say they do not feel alive without their drug of choice.

Mankind is reaching a point where we have to decide if we are humans or animals. It is time to make the choice of the spirit of God or continue to live in darkness. Do you want to reawaken the essence of man and find the unity and power we are predestined to have? There are steps you can take to awaken and recognize your true self.

A New Age of God

Jesus is the light and He will lead you! All He asks is for you to follow and it will come to pass. In the following sections of this book we will cover the steps to help you find a closer walk with the Creator and to relocate that essence of God that still waits within waiting to be rekindled. Through the salvation of Jesus and the guidance of the Holy Spirit you can put away the old person and be renewed into a new being in Christ. Only through the Father can we cast off the old rags of the old man and be dressed in the new clothes.

> **Isaiah 45:4-8.** *I call you by name though you do not know me. I have surnamed you. I am the one and only God; none other. I form the light. I do all things: let righteousness rain down.*

We all have a true name that only God knows and we receive that name when we receive our salvation and become the new man in Christ. It is time to start taking off the old rags and begin to assume the life of the new man.

We will talk about the value of meditation on God, spoken prayer and giving praise to the Lord and how that process will awaken the voice within. God has implanted within each of us a spark of the infinite in each of His children and it resides in your heart. It will begin to awaken your spiritual voice and you will start to gradually evolve. You will begin to be bolder in your faith, and in knowing what you want out of life.

God is the bonfire and you are a spark off of the fire. You will smolder without fuel to feed the fire. The Holy Spirit is that fuel to take your spark that feeds you to become a part of the cleansing fire. Your priorities will gradually begin to change both on the inside and in how you will

A New Age of God

perceive your life. As your awareness of self begins to grow, you will also become more aware of the world and see how the media and your daily surroundings strive to keep you distracted. The goal of the world is to keep you absorbed in their cycle of madness. The more strife in the world, the more distracted everyone becomes and they drift farther and farther from their true nature and fall into the trap of the conscious mind that believes only what can be seen. The majority of people can no longer think for themselves which means they have lost the ability to discern.

The enemy of man wants you self-centered and trying to keep up with the Joneses, to keep you working so hard you will stay preoccupied so you will ignore your children, your life and your faith. They keep you wound up in your emotions and ego. Satan is the king of I, me and my; and he uses your ego as the doorway to wreak havoc on your life so he can keep you in strife.

Mankind is suffering from a disease that I call; the, "Me" disease. All I hear from people is me, me, and me over and over again. That was the downfall of Lucifer who put himself above all else and waged a war to win God's throne. There is something greater than me, greater than you and true happiness comes from that realization; all that we are comes from the Father and without Him we are but animations of life lived in one dimension just like the reflection.

Jesus lived a life of absolute faith so we could witness and learn. He had a faith that could calm the storm and the seas. By faith and by word He told the elements, peace be still and the seas clamed. The Apostles wondered what type man is this that can work this miracle. It is apparent all through the New Testament that Jesus tried to communicate who He was and what He came to do. Still they kept asking Him when they would see the Messiah.

A New Age of God

Their rational minds could not grasp who Jesus was and why He came to the earth.

If the people who walked with Jesus had trouble having faith, understanding and believing then we should not be so hard ourselves when we fail to meet the standards we try to achieve. All you need to do is admit (recognize) you stumbled, tell God you know you have erred (be convicted) acknowledge that and sincerely try to learn from your mistake (ask forgiveness) and move on in grace.

That is the most tremendous thing about Jesus; He is a forgiving God that wants you to learn and grow in your faith. You are His child and He wants you to learn from your mistakes and become a better person.

> **Romans 10:9-10.** *If you will confess with your mouth to the Lord Jesus, and you will believe in you heart that God has raised Him from the dead, you will be saved. For with the heart man believes onto righteousness; and with the mouth confession is made onto salvation.*

When you decide to pursue a new way of life in Christ, you are just like someone who is training for their first marathon; they could not run 26 miles when they began to train. Faith mixes with the word and is ingested within the self and that feeds your faith; which strengthens your faith. This process works like a magneto driving a dynamo, increasing in speed and force to build your faith.

To have faith is to know the power of the word; when you believe in knowing you create and receive; accept what you receive with joy and faith. You will begin to see you are finding favor with the Lord. Once you start receiving what is rightfully yours you will be upset you wasted so much of your life.

A New Age of God

Every prayer moves you to a closer level with the Lord, with each petition the Lord dispatches an Angel to help you receive what you need. When you sing His praises you get His undivided attention; you bypass the Angels and you receive direct action from the Lord. Praise brings the Lords focus to you and He can speak directly to you.

When you live in the unity of faith, it will heal you and nothing will have dominion over you for you will no longer live in separation from the Father of us all.

> **James 1:17** *Every good gift and every perfect gift is from above, and comes down from the Father of lights, with whom there is no variableness, neither shadow of turning.*

Belief means you know with all your heart that you receive and accept. Your belief should be as a little child; a child believes with doubt and get so excited about what he is about to receive. A child can taste it before they eat it and they can see it before they receive it. If you believe that Jesus is the son of God and the Bible is the word of God; then trust in the Lord with your heart and mind. The people of God are always on the clock for God. If you pray, say and do for God you will have an awakening in your Spirit and your life will have more contentment. You will start to receive more and more God's love. That is why God is calling you, so you may live in grace and receive the gifts of God.

There develops a connected relationship that is unceasing. There is a synchronicity between loving and being loved. One love, one life, and one spirit in unity; that over comes the chaos of this world; that is the Jesus Way. The enemy is the master of distraction, always trying to keep you separated from God.

A New Age of God

You must be in control of your emotions, in control of your actions and focused on what is your greatest goal. Pay careful attention to what the media puts out for your supposed entertainment. There is a hidden agenda so the world will be desensitized by violence, language and sex which are being poured into your mind through television, music, movies and games in the name of entertainment. If you accept these things as the norm then you will accept what they are planning for the world.

The military uses the video games that children play to train young soldiers to be able to kill. They want to eliminate the natural instinct that it is wrong to kill so they will be more effective in times of war. These are the same games our kids are playing in their bedrooms. We are training a generation that the gun is the solution to any kind of conflict and we are opening them up to influences that would have been unthinkable twenty years ago. This is why there are so many school shootings and why the disgruntled employee or estranged spouse takes the gun to work to settle their problems. What have you been allowing in your home?

We are spirit beings in Earthly form from and we have been seduced by the world to ignore our spirit half. We each are meant to make a spirit walk on the Jesus Way. This means we need to be living a spirit filled life. Do you have an aching and longing in your inner being and you can't figure what is wrong? I give you my word you are aching for the life you were created to live.

To achieve the life the Creator meant you to have you must first quiet the earthly urges and feed the spirit so it may grow. Residing within is the God Spark that has been with you since before you were born. This is the ember planted within the Spirit that holds the flame of the passion of God. When a baby is born it has a pure spirit and most small children see angels and talk with

A New Age of God

them before the rational world blinds their spiritual eyes and the rational world smothers the spirit side.

Our life is meant to be a spirit walk for which we are predestined. Planted deep within of each person the spark of God lies awaiting the flame to ignite the spark into gently burning flame and through worship we can grow a limitless love. The Holy Spirit is the keeper of the flame and is waiting for your request to grow into a guiding presence that flows from God and resides within. Your Spirit needs to be fed by the Holy Spirit so it may blossom through its connection with God. Prayer, praise and meditation feed the flame of faith and your faith builds your praise, prayer and meditation. It is a cycle of worship that is designed to lead you into the purpose you came to achieve.

Prayer, Praise and Meditation

When you pray you are reaching out to God; when you praise you are sending out your love and devotion to God; and when you meditate you are focusing on God and being still so you may listen. Meditation is essential because how can you hear an answer if you don't quiet your mind and listen? Each cycle of devotion is like forging a golden link in the chain that connects you with the Lord. You are creating a link that cannot be broken and with each prayer the chain grows and becomes stronger. This builds your temple within. The Lord told the Pharisees that if they tore down this temple He could raise it in three days. He was talking about Himself as a temple. When God speaks of building a church or a temple He is talking about the kingdom within. It is our responsibility to build and honor the temple within. This requires daily devotion and work; it is not a part time labor. It is the most vital labor of this life.

> *Faith grows, stand in faith, develop your faith and it will manifest.*

One life, one love, one Spirit unified is the reality. This is the life we were designed for and until we learn to live the life God wants us to manifest we will continue to live in denial and allow the strife of the world to affect us.

The Spirit of Rebellion

> **John 3:19.** *And this is the condemnation, that the Light has come into the world, and men loved the darkness rather than light, because their deeds were evil. John 3:21. For every one that does evil hates the light neither comes to the light, lest his deeds be reproved (revealed and judged).*

Rebellious and defiant people suffer and struggle to find their way in the world. They are constantly defying authority, talking about how unfair life is and looking for an easy out of the responsibilities of life. If you are defiant will have to toil all your life and live in aloneness and separation. You will not grow in spirit, as the body wears out and the back fails because it cannot carry the load any longer. You will feel like you have no back up in your life, because you refuse to reach out to others and refuse to acknowledge God. They refuse to ask Him to reach down and give them what is needed. When you choose to walk alone and live by your own rules you are opening yourself and your family to the mercy of the enemy. The enemy's favorite recreation is toying with the life of unbelievers.

Obedience

> **John 3:21.** *But he that does truth comes to the light that by his deeds may made manifest, that they are wrought in God.*

God's obedient children live for God's presence in their life will be guided by His light and will walk under Grace and will find the favor of the Father of Mankind. Your good works for God will manifest great things into your life. You are meant to be the Children of the Almighty God. Yours is the walk of the Spirit on Earth. You are not a fleshly body with a soul but a Spirit person with the body of a man. Love and obedience are the keys to finding favor with the Lord. He always responds to faithfulness and devotion.

> **Ephesians 6:12-13.** *For we wrestle not against flesh and blood, but against principalities, against powers, against the rulers of the darkness of this world, against spiritual wickedness in high places. Wherefore take unto the whole armor of God, that ye may be able to withstand in the evil day, having done all, to stand.*

Your problems are not caused by any one man, a bad job or whatever you think is your problem. The real fight is on the spiritual plane fighting the darkness of the world. The enemy has many servants in his army and men that serve him in the name of fame and money. He has people in charge of the media, the movie producers and Wall Street. You need to open your eyes and see the truth that you are being bombarded with influences of darkness. They want you to believe it is all pretend and fantasy

A New Age of God

but they are working to infiltrate you mind through your subconscious.

To overcome the poison of the enemy; overcome the lies of mankind and heal your mind, body and soul we must first recognize the problem, know our enemy and know how to fight the enemy. This is vital to subduing the animal within, stopping outside influences and living in God. All we are meant to be is achievable through God and you need to walk in oneness with Most High God and see the light that is there to guide you. His wisdom is the light and if you seek His light, He will guide you through the darkness.

> **Matthew 12:29-30.** *Or how else can a man enter into a strong man's house, and spoil his goods, except he first bind the strong man? And then he will spoil his house. He that is not with Me is against Me; he that gathers not with me scatters abroad.*

If you stand strong in the Lord you can withstand all comers but if you stand alone following your emotions, you will be blown to the four winds. All you are is because God created you for a life of the spirit of God flourishing within. You were a spirit with God in heaven before you were born upon the Earth; uniquely designed for your specific talents and with a destiny. You will continue in spirit after this life of the flesh; this existence is but a blink of the eye of eternity. You are a spirit eternal. You are not an accident; you might have been a surprise to your parents but nothing surprises God.

Oneness of purpose, of love and focus

What you see is not all there is! When you look in the mirror you know there is more to you than a one dimensional reflection of the self. What lies within is not reflected by the mirror, it does not show who you are, just your image. That is what you see every day is a mere reflection of the glory; it does not show what created it. The mirror doesn't show what makes the heartbeat, what the eyes see; you cannot see with earthly eyes the magic that lies hidden to be sought out by the true seekers.

Seekers of the truth will uncover the miracles but those just seeking knowledge will not be able to open the door.

The blind will not see; the dead of spirit cannot live! You are meant to be alive in and see with a vision of spiritual eyes. When Adam and Eve ate the forbidden fruit of knowledge (it wasn't an apple!), it poisoned the spirit of man and veiled his eyes to seeing the spiritual splendor of his life with God. This is how the veil between God and man came into existence

The change was immediate and they began to see everything with the eyes of the carnal man and they lost communion with God. They fell, dominated by the senses and ruled by their urges. They felt shame where it had never been before; they felt guilt for the first time. Because they had defied God and ruined their pure essence they had to leave paradise and walk a life on earth. Not only themselves but all their offspring had to pay the price of disobedience. The original sin of the garden is a generational curse and is passed down through the generations and you must break that curse and work to reawaken the spirit.

Jesus came to the world to bring a new kingdom. Satan had infiltrated the Pharisees and was dominating the world and Jesus came to show mankind the way out.

A New Age of God

The Priests had the ability provide atonement for the sins of the people which covered and postponed the sin for another year but did not provide forgiveness. In just bought one more year of favor for the people. Jesus came and provided forgiveness which wiped the slate clean so the sins of the past no longer existed. The new kingdom Jesus' preached about was the kingdom of the Father within.

If you have had tremendous trials and had tragedies befall you let it be the fire that has made you into who you are today. Being bitter or resentful only hurts you more and more every day and keeps you bound in the past, you can relive it but you cannot go back and change the past. The best thing you can do is to make it your responsibility to use those tragic events to help others heal and cope or prevent someone from going through what you went through. They might not be as strong as you and you could save them from drowning in pain and regret.

Faith comes by saying the word and by doing. The obedience of doing grows your faith.

The act of obedience stands you in faith and the daily practice of using the word will develop your faith. Growing your faith moves you towards manifesting what you want to pass. For what you want already is already created in heaven and your faith brings it into being for you. You are building the pathway to flourish and become stronger so we may establish favor and grace of God.

The Holy Spirit is Comforter and our guide and only the one who can guide us to our purpose. We are created for a purpose and we must connect with that guidance so we will have wisdom (which comes from God) to recognize opportunity. Please realize God will not force this upon you, He is a gentleman that is waiting on your request, which is why you have free will. Everything is there waiting for you, but it is up to you to make the choice.

Windows of opportunity

We all make mistakes in life, which is part of growing and learning how to live. As we move through life we are given windows of opportunity in which God offers us a helping hand to move us forward in the proper direction. Each time we casually walk past this opening into our future the opportunity closes behind us. It might come as some inspiring person who moves to change our thinking or how we see our life. Perhaps a new career opens up for you but you would have to start over and take the risk, and you would be required to step out in faith.

Stepping out in faith

God is always trying to move us forward. If you are not moving and growing you are falling behind. Taking a step out in faith always requires you to move out of your comfort zone. If you do not move out of your comfort zone you will not grow. God wants you to always be moving forward and growing. That is why anything that challenges you requires an act of faith on your behalf and God will carry you through. Nothing worth doing is easy or comfortable but the reward is your growth in confidence in yourself and in your faith that God is with you in all you do. If God is for you then who can stand against you?

When we go through life these portals of opportunity await us. Each time we ignore these portals, we stray from our path and we diverge farther and farther from the true path of our life. If you are going through life feeling like

A New Age of God

you are swimming upstream every day and nothing comes easy then you are not flowing in the stream of life. Ever noticed how artists and musicians talk about getting into the flow of creativity? They are listening to their higher creative voice and they are allowing it to flow. When you ignore your inner voice and follow your blind emotions you are going against your spirit walk and are in danger of opening yourself to unwanted turmoil. The inner guidance is there to keep you safe and on your path.

One of the hardest things to do is to understand we are not our emotions. Emotions are separate things and are driven by the conscious mind generated to keep us in our comfort zone or to feed our egos. When you follow your emotions and the urges of the flesh you will live your life like a dog obsessed with catching its tail. You will go in circles trying to keep that emotional high, which is an emotional addiction that can lead to drugs and alcohol to try to maintain that level of emotion.

That inner recording in your head will lead you around by the nose and can destroy relationships and eventually ruin your life. If you need to do something to make you feel important or superior to be happy then you are living off your emotions. If you hate someone because of the color of their skin or their religion and feel they are inferior to you then you are allowing the enemy to rule your ego and emotions to keep you in the bondage of hate and self-righteousness.

There is the woman who spends her life looking for romance and never keep a relationship because they can't keep her in that romantic glow every day of her life. Then there's the man, whose image relies on the woman on his arm or the car he drives. He is always looking for his next ex-wife to keep him young because he is never satisfied with what he has in his life.

A New Age of God

The faster you try to run from God, the harder your life will try to stop you, turn you around and get you back on your path. The stronger your fight, the harder life will become and eventually you will be on your knees begging God for guidance to get back to some sort of peace in your life.

How much peace is there is for someone in an abusive relationship? Do you think the alcoholic or drug addict has any peace in their life? When the police are at the door, when child welfare shows up for the kids or when choices they have made leaves them without true friends or family; one day they wake up and find themselves crying out to God asking what happened; how could this have happened? How did they get to that place in your life? What do you need to change and make some sense of your life? Once their life is in ruins they blame God for their mess instead of taking responsibility for their actions and changing their lives. We have a tendency to rationalize our actions and make excuses for the choices we have made that have put our lives in chaos.

This may seem like extreme examples but I promise you people get into that position; they fight the system, break the laws of man and God then they wind up crying out in the dark of night for help.

Miracles happen; Jesus can cure addictions and heal the hurts of a lifetime. All you have to do is turn to God; HE can cure anything!

Starting Over

Jesus can give you a start over, no matter what you have done; He can erase the past and allow you to make a new start. I know because it happened to me; God changed me into a new person. My life was in the tank and I couldn't see a way out. I was living in complete darkness.

A New Age of God

It was Christmas morning I was in despair, deeply depressed and the enemy had me convinced I was trapped in a marriage and a life that I couldn't get out of. I took about a hundred assorted pills consisting of antidepressants and tranquilizers. The doctors had had me on pills pills to get me going, tranquilizers to bring me back down, antidepressants and pain pills. I was so medicated I could no longer feel God and felt isolated and alone. I was so miserable that the act of living actually hurt. I couldn't see any reason to go on living in hell on earth. All I wanted was to find peace in oblivion. My husband came home from the bars in Mexico just as I was fading away into oblivion and his solution was to try to beat me awake which resulted in some bruises and broken fingers, when I was unresponsive he decided to get me to the hospital. They tell me I died 3 times while they were working on me and I was in a coma for 3 days. They said I would never recover and if I did I would have irreparable brain damage.

They say the Lord chooses the most unlikely people to do his work. That is how you know it is the work of God and not man…Suddenly I was in a beautiful garden; the largest trees I had ever seen swayed gently in a soft breeze. They surrounded a large lake that was so clear it was like a mirror reflecting the trees. I was standing in tall green emerald grass beside a babbling stream that fed into the lake. The aroma of the air was filled with the scent of hundreds of different flowers and for the first time ever I was comfortable within myself and I had a total sense of peace, as I started to walk I came around a bend in the path and was greeted by a 7 foot tall man with wavy shoulder length light brown hair and twinkling blue eyes. With a sweet smile he greeted me as if we were old friends and we began walking and talking like old friends.

A New Age of God

I felt as if I had always known him and felt completely safe and secure. I had always been uneasy around other people especially strangers, always feeling like I didn't quite measure up and they would soon realize I was a phony and reject me but here all those feelings were completely gone. I felt like I had finally found my way home after a long journey. We walked along the shore of the lake and he began to speak to me about how valuable my life was and how much I was loved.

He spoke of all the times my guides and guardians had moved to protect me and save me from myself, but this time I had gone too far. I remembered all the times my conscience warned me against my actions but I would ignore them and go along with the group trying to be accepted and loved. I was always trying to make everyone happy but I was always in misery within myself. I had always felt like I was like one of those chocolate figures that looked perfect on the outside but they are completely hollow inside.

He showed me all the possibilities I had thrown away, making destructive decisions, never seeing any value in anything or myself and suddenly I began to see how I had trashed my life and wasting all the gifts God had waiting for me. I had allowed the doctors to medicate myself to the point not even God could reach me. The medication had altered my ability to make rational choices and the Deceiver had almost won, but Jesus in His grace had interceded to help me see what I was doing with my life.

What an imitation of life I had been leading, I was a spiritual wasteland wandering in the desert. I saw and felt how I was grieving the Holy Spirit. I was given gifts and talents and there was a purpose to my life. I was not living a life, but existing in death. Drugs, sex and alcohol were dragging me farther and farther down into darkness.

A New Age of God

The seeds of deceit that had been planted in my life as a child had robbed me of the vision I was intended to have.

> **Romans 5:5** *and hope make not ashamed; because the love of God is not shed abroad in our hearts by the Holy Ghost which is given unto us.*

It became clear that how I was raised was not an excuse and what I had done was grieving the Holy Spirit who had tried to reach out to so many times in my life and I had ignored the inner voice as words of desperation from my imagination. I understood with absolute clarity what was really important and I began to see what life was truly about. I had spent my entire life feeling unworthy, unwanted and unloved.

I never felt wanted by my parents; I was shifted to one relative or the other for as long as they would have me. I rarely went a complete year in one school and my teachers thought we were migrant workers. I was out of school and pregnant at 15. The next child was born when I was 18 and I gave them both up because I felt I was not good enough to raise my two children, both were born outside of marriage, neither man wanted me or his child.

I had no education and I didn't have the love and support of a family to help me to grow up and figure out what was expected of me. It was devastating to give up my babies but I wanted them to grow up loved and cared for and I felt I had nothing to offer them. I didn't think anyone would ever love me. I felt they were better off without me and their only chance in this world would be with anyone else raising them.

When I gave up my precious daughter for adoption I started drinking and using drugs to stop the guilt and the pain. Three years later I realized I was pregnant again

A New Age of God

it was the wakeup call to stop the drugs. Unfortunately I didn't stop the drinking and I harmed my baby in the process. He has had problems all his life from the effects of the alcohol. It is amazing how much guilt a person can live with and still pretend to survive. I felt so unworthy that I had my tubes tied so I could never have another child.

Now I came to realize that I am loved beyond words, I had a Father that loved me above all else and He has expectations and a purpose for my life. I was not an imposition to Him but someone who loved me enough to send guardians to protect me. It still brings me to tears to know I am loved so very much. I am truly loved.

All was not lost; even though I had committed one of the greatest sins, with Jesus' grace and love I still had a choice in the matter; I could go back and live for my life for God or I could stay there and proceed to the throne of judgment but I would not be allowed to remain; once I had reviewed my life, and gave witness to all I had done and what I had not done then I would be separated from paradise. I could forfeit all the love and grace I had found at last and live in separation from all the ones that loved me and wanted to see me succeed in this life. He was offering me mercy and salvation.

I chose to accept God's love and come back and try to do it right. I immediately began to weep and ask God to forgive me. I asked to be given a second chance to do Gods work and will. I knew exactly what I had to do and knew how to do it. Everything was perfectly clear to me. I felt cleansed and purified; no longer a second class citizen but a child of the Most High God.

When I awoke there was no brain damage and I had a completely new personality. I had a new outlook on life, I saw with new eyes and felt like a whole new person. Many of my friends and family said I was a different person.

A New Age of God

One friend who professed to be a physic said she believed the old me had died and a new spirit had inhabited my body. How right she was because God had remade me! I don't think she understood what she had actually said because she had not yet found Christ in her life. She had no frame of reference to understand what had happened to me.

The hopelessness was gone; I had an inner strength that I had never felt before. How can you explain what it feels like to live a life in which you feel unloved and unwanted and suddenly you know you are special and that you are loved? All I can say is, I never wanted to grieve Jesus again no matter what I had to do. There was no honor or fidelity in my marriage and I knew I had to end it and start my life anew. When I looked at the man I had married it was if I were looking at a stranger. He had contributed to my trashing my life and making me feel like I was living in hell. It took a while to get free of all the bondage and build a new life, but within two years God in His grace sent me the wonderful man I have been with for the last 35 years.

I don't care what your situation, or what your life is like, God is there for you too and you can change anything through Him. Reach out to Jesus from a prison cell or a penthouse, the distance is the same. He knows your life, He knows your pain. If you want to know what Jesus wants I can tell you because He told me that He loves you beyond the words and knowing of man! Jesus wants you to be triumphant. He wants you to live in joy. He wants you to walk with Him every day. He wants you to know you are perfect. He loves you so much that He suffered the sins of the world for you. He sits at the right hand of God right now with the scars of the crucifixion on His body.

A New Age of God

Jesus said that all that He did on Earth you too can do. If you have faith and walk with God, you can operate in the spirit and utilize the gifts of the Holy Spirit. This is the life you were intended to live. He will forgive and give you a new life.

God will give you His grace; you can have His salvation if you ask. If you will open your heart to the Lord, He will start to become a part of your life. You too can wake up to a new life and a new purpose. He can heal all the damage you have done to your body and your mind. He can remake you and your life.

All you have to do is pray for the Lord to come into your life, to forgive you for your past. Speak sincerely from your heart, state your belief in Jesus and that you believe He died for your salvation and tell Jesus how you feel and be sincere in you petition. This will start the most amazing transition of your life.

Sometimes it comes suddenly and other times it is a slow transition into a new way of feeling and thinking. However this happens it will start the most amazing transformation you have ever experienced. That is why some born again Christians bother others so much. They are so excited by their experience that they want everyone to share in their joy but sometimes something bad thing happens, evil sneaks in and implant a spirit of self-righteousness, and they start to judge and feel superior to the initiated. They expect everyone's experience to be just like theirs and they think that how they arrived there is the way everyone should be. They want you to see the world with their eyes and live as they live. The Lord deals with everyone according to their perceptions and their needs.

There is one God and He is the Father of us all and His Son, Jesus Christ intercedes for and forgives. He sends us the Holy Spirit who guides each person according to their

A New Age of God

needs. He has many children of many races and customs that He loves equally. Each of us has their own path and culturally diversified ways of expressing their worship. All prayer, praise and worship are equally received in heaven. If music is played and sung in praise it is Holy in intent and received by God equally.

As Christians we have a responsibility to offer a helping hand to anyone that is down. It is easy to condemn and criticize those who are down and lost but if we are to be the body of Christ we must step up and reach out to help our brothers. We must try to emulate Him in everything we do. We are representatives of the Most High and it is a serious responsibility. The Lord deals with us all in our own manner that relates to our culture. He is our creator and He knows how to relate to each of us as individuals because we all precious and equal in the eyes of the Lord.

The goal is to awaken your faith through love, faith and worship. To live the life you were intended to live. You are learning how to build a life led in partnership with God through the love and inspiration of the Holy Spirit. The most integral part of this awakening is the power of the spoken word. What you say matters and influences your mind and what you say determines the direction of your life. It is vital you learn the power of the spoken word because it can be a powerful gift or a terrible curse. You have the power to create or the power to destroy or limit your life. We all hold the power to heal old wounds that have held mankind back for generations. We are His hands and they can be hands of healing if we choose to take His path.

CHAPTER 2

The Calling

Acts 2:39. *The promise is unto you, and to your children, and to all that are far off, even as many as the Lord our God will call.*

The Lord is calling His children to come into unity and start to do the works of God. This isn't a calling for everyone to become a Methodist, a Baptist, Catholic, Latter Day Saint, etc. This is a calling for people to recognize that they came to this world to walk with the Lord and agreed to work towards our purpose.

In the beginning we all lived as spirits on the God plane and we agreed to come here for specific purposes. Only through the Holy Spirit can we come to know that purpose. That is why God is calling you to bring you into unity so you can come to know your true nature as well as your purpose.

Our God does not recognize denominations that strive to dictate what is the will and law of God. We have been given a guide book and that is the Bible which is the word of God. The Bible was written to show us how to live. It

A New Age of God

is full of stories meant to teach and inspire us. When we read and comprehend through the Holy Spirit you will begin to comprehend with new understanding. Believing there is only one way to worship God is a lie of Satan to keep us separated into factions so we will keep judging each other instead of embracing our brothers and sisters of humanity. There is no one true religion, just one true God. Jesus did not suffer and die to give you a religion!

Our God is a supernatural God and He will not be minimalized to one hour on Sunday! He is the way and the light and we must begin our journey with the Jesus. I am calling for you to learn the Tao (the way or the road) of Jesus.

Wars have been waged in the name of Christianity and so many well intentioned spiritual leaders have driven off entire cultures because they see the way of Christ to be the way it has always been since the European influence created the church and reformed and remade the church to represent their ideals and perceptions and turned it into religion. They have dictated what you have to wear, what music to worship to and how you must behave in worship. Time has come folks to break the bondage of man's interpretations and be free to worship God with you heart and your very being. The hour has come for you to learn the basic methods of reaching out to God and building a life of joy and freedom.

Don't misunderstand me, if you are a Catholic, Baptist or any other denomination and you are happy there I am happy for you, all I'm saying is you can't claim it to be the only way to worship. Having a spiritual family and having a teacher of the word is an important part of your life to assist you with your walk in Christ.

It is possible to stand alone and at times you may have to but it is much easier to have the help and support of family. I want this to be a way for you to grow in your

A New Age of God

faith. If you haven't been to church in years or have never been to church I hope this will help you find your path to a church home. It is like trying to find a good pair of shoes that feel just right. You might have to try on a few to find the right place of worship.

There is a world that lies within Jesus that most of the traditional churches have failed to bring to the people. You can have a relationship with Christ regardless of ethnicity, your cultural background or past. Whatever you have been taught you about matters of God, you can take the next step into a deeper relationship with Jesus Christ. Jesus is limitless... lets work together to remove the limits from your life. If we live a limitless life we can live without the separation that exists between the tribes of man.

The first Nations of the world have a deep spiritual heritage and can have as close a relationship with the creator as anyone else. It is their right to express their love and devotion within their own cultural heritage and language. Innumerable souls have been lost from the touch of Christ because of the self-righteousness of the European style missionaries who taught that to follow Christ they had to abandon their culture and their language and become images of the missionaries to live as a Christian. I believe that is why there is such alcoholism and poverty within the Native American nation because they have become trapped between two worlds and there is a confusion of the spirit that does not allow them to be at peace with themselves and the world. I believe that only through the Holy Spirit can we heal the hurts of the past and learn to walk in brotherhood.

We must work to resolve old wounds and embrace each other as brothers and sisters in Christ living our lives in honesty and honor. It is time to reach out and help each other rather than dwell on the pain of the past and recognize the lies that keep us separated. We have so much to offer each other and if we are to heal the world we must start with healing old wounds and misconceptions about each other.

Language is just a means of communication, praise is praise regardless of language it reaches the heart and mind of God and it moves your life. God does not care how you dress or wear your hair. What He cares about is your heart and how you live your life. How you praise, pray and worship comes from within, springing from your heart not from my guidelines or from anyone else.

God talks to you and you should reply in your own way. You were created by the Father of us All, in perfection for you to be where you are and be proud of who you are. If you are true to yourself in worship to the one true God, honor your culture and background and God will rejoice with you.

People always talk about finding themselves and understanding the secret to life, well I believe we are all created to live in love, honor our families and our cultures so we may live in oneness with each other through the Father. You should not have to leave your culture behind and change to follow this guide to build your worship. All steps towards unity with God should be celebrated. Faith is the foundation in a life in Christ.

If you live in India, China or if you are a member of one of the First Nations (the list of peoples of the world is endless) your basic culture is a deep part of you that should be honored with pride and your traditions honored. Following the way of Jesus is just a completion of the self. We all are destined to make a spirit walk on this planet to fulfill our destiny.

The world in which we live consists of much more than can be seen with your mortal eyes. This is proven in the

A New Age of God

world of microbes and viruses which exist even though they cannot be seen with the human eye. Science has proven atoms are influenced by outside forces and scientists are attempting to explain the universe through quantum physics.

You are a Devine creation of God that survives this life, your spirit is indestructible, and a life force that passes to another state when the body expires. While we are here God wants us to live in peace, and exist with a relationship with God and live in the light of oneness. God is the light, and it is up to us to attune ourselves with intent, faith and love. We are meant to walk with God, do his works in all things.

The law was given to man as a guide to show the way man was to live, but the truth is we cannot live as directed without Christ to guide us. The Old Testament is there to prophesize the coming of Christ and to lead you into the New Testament. We must work from the inside to the outside so we can be more like Him.

True righteousness

You have a body and a soul but you are a creature of spirit. Once your spirit joins with the Holy Spirit you are reborn as a whole person in Christ. You cannot walk in your own righteousness because it comes from the self and the ego.

Once you are born again in the spirit you begin to accept the nature of God and start your walk in His righteousness. You become a part of the body of Christ and He will begin the work within. Once you accept and receive salvation your faith will grow by hearing the word of God and you become established in righteousness. We cannot live a righteous life on our own but through Christ we are righteous through Him that dwells within. In God's eyes we are complete but only through the Holy Spirit can we live Christ's completeness.

> **Romans 10:1-3.** *Brethren my heart's desire and my prayer to God for Israel (man), is that they be saved. I bear them record that they have the zeal (heart) of God, but not according to knowledge. For them being ignorant of God's righteousness, and going about to establish their own righteousness, have not submitted to the righteousness of God. Christ is the end of the law for righteousness to everyone that believes.*

The righteousness of God comes from Christ through the Holy Spirit. You cannot have it on your own you must take Jesus' righteousness for your own. Righteousness, faith and love are forces that come from Christ. Without Christ you cannot defeat the voice of Satan whose works are to keep us walking in condemnation. Condemnation is a disease of the spirit that will erode your faith just like a cancer eating the body.

The enemy wants us to keep reliving our mistakes and keep us in sin consciousness. When we allow our minds to constantly relive our mistakes we stay in sin consciousness which destroys our faith and we start to doubt who we really are and how we should think and act. The devils job is to keep us in doubt which keeps us separated from the Father of us all. Until you are right with God and understand righteousness Satan will continue to reign in your life and wreak havoc in your life.

Once you accept Christ's salvation you become a part of Him. You become a new person in Christ that has no past and your slate is clean. That is why Jesus renamed His

A New Age of God

disciples when they chose to follow Christ. Saul was the greatest persecutor of Christians until on the Damascus road God shined the light of heaven down and blinded him. It took that extreme action to get someone this devoted to the destruction of the Christians to listen to the voice of God.

Saul was a devout man who believed he was doing the work of God but he had been led astray by the teachings of the Pharisees. Christ took that zeal for God and turned Saul into Paul and he became the greatest Apostle. Christ cleaned away his past, renamed him and remade him into a new man with a new name and a new purpose! To what length will God have to go to reach you?

You and I are a part of Him (the body of Christ). When we walk with the presence of the Holy Spirit within we have a new life with a new purpose and a new destination. We need to allow the presence of the Holy Spirit to come forth in all we do and we cannot allow the doubt and the condemnation of other to affect our walk in Christ. Christ is the shield to defeat Satan.

When people from our past start bring up who you were before Christ that is the enemy using them to bring you into sin consciousness. They are living in past condemnation and they want you to stay there with them. These are people that will refuse the hand which Jesus is extending to the world and they do not want you to walk in Christ either. They want you to stay in the old life in the old ways.

That is why it is essential for you to forgive yourself and release the past so you cannot be drug back into that old person. It is essential to understand completely that you are delivered from that life and you need to walk away from that life and only focus on the new life. Just tell yourself when the past encroaches on your mind that you feel sorry for that old man walking in his rags and

A New Age of God

darkness but that is no longer who you are. Think of that old man as another person and do not take ownership of what was erased through the grace and mercy of Jesus.

When we feel guilt or regret, dwelling in the past and we lose the righteousness of Christ and begin to relive those things that we have given to Jesus when we accepted His forgiveness and His salvation. To dwell in the past is to reject His forgiveness and call it back into your life.

When you live in regret or guilt you are putting back on the old rags of sin and you cannot wear two sets of clothes at once. If you want to wear the robes of righteousness you must cast off the old rags of the past. No weapon formed against you can succeed.

There is a divinity that we are meant to have and we can live in such righteousness that sickness and disease cannot live in our bodies. It will have no right to touch your body or affect your health. The same thing that Jesus had within Him, we have the same within us when we receive the Holy Spirit. I want what Jesus had and I will live my life to have the same force to manifest in my life and I want you to have this same life. The walk with the Holy Spirit begins through salvation.

The first and most vital key to unity with God is love.

God loves you with a love that is unending. Imagine you have three children who you love unconditionally and one day one of them loses their way and does not come home. Imagine the agony and heartache you would suffer as you try to find your child to bring it home. That is how God feels about each of us that are living in the darkness of separation. He desperately wants you to come home to Him. He is calling out to you, desperate for you to be

A New Age of God

home safe in His arms. You are His child; He created you out of love above all His other creations. You are His chosen one, created especially for a purpose. His original plan was for man to walk side by side with Him in perfection.

Jesus came here in human form to show us how to overcome the limitations of this life and get back to our relationship with the creator. He was considered such a heretic the teachings of the Pharisees and His radical views went against their ideals to the point they turned their backs on Him and incited Him to be crucified. They did not realize what they had was done to fulfill the prophecy of the Messiah.

What have we lost over the ages since Jesus walked the land? His teachings say we can have anything if we just trust in the Father. You may have been taught the ways of your earthly father's house but if you believe in Jesus, you are a part of His Fathers family and you must learn the ways of His house and start to live by the covenants He has put forth for each and every one of His children.

You must to choose how you want to live. You cannot continue to follow the world and its propaganda because if you do you will no longer be following the leadership of Jesus. No man can serve two masters, if you choose to follow Christ you will leave the ways and workings of the world behind. You are standing at the crossroads and you must decide which direction your life should take.

Do you want to ignore the calling of God and just keep on living in the status quo? Before you decide how you want to live come spend some time with me so you have a chance to make an educated decision about your life and how you want to spend eternity.

Come with me and see if you begin to change your conception of the world around you. If you keep an open

A New Age of God

heart and mind you can change your mind for the better, you can change the altitude of your thoughts and your belief will increase; with belief comes faith and your reach will grow closer and closer to God.

Please give me your time and read this, try the process I recommend and see if it talks to your heart. Walk with me for 90 days and see if you don't get into a better understanding of the state of your mind and how you are living your life. Within a year you will see the miracle of a life in Christ to begin to manifest in your life! Things that seemed so difficult will become simple and your life will start to fall into place.

My prayer is for you to fall in unconditional love with Jesus and I want you to fall in love with a new life on the Jesus Way. All things will be possible! I want you to be amazed with the real life you can lead with Jesus and stop existing in an illusion.

It has taken me 30 years of seeking to compile this process and this information. Only in the last year has God put the desire in my heart to share this with you. One of the biggest secrets I have learned in the last year is obedience. I have learned to be obedient to His requests and guidance and it has opened the door to more and more guidance.

Before I started to compile this book I felt I was being called by God to move but I didn't understand in what direction I was being led. I just didn't understand what I was supposed to be doing. I went on a ten day fast with prayer and meditation to dedicate myself to do the will of God. I promised God that I would do whatever he directed me to do. I had written numerous essays on subjects that the Lord had spoken to me about over the years but I never considered writing a book.

A New Age of God

I quit my job, devoted myself to my spiritual work and this book is the result. You too can find your calling and move by the direction of the Holy Spirit to find your calling and grow in spirit. Make no promises you do not intend to keep, because God always keeps His covenants and He expects no less of His children.

The church has done the world a disservice by limiting their teachings of Jesus and this has limited the vision of man and their ability to grow within the vision that God has for them. The church has been dominated by people who want to intellectualize God. They want to secularize the word of God and take the supernatural side away. You cannot know God through the reason of the mind. You are required to bypass the mind and understand through the heart the things of the spirit. They have separated the people from God and instead of helping people walk within the Holy Spirits guidance; they are teaching a limited relationship. God is not just empty words spoken on Sunday morning and then you have done your lip service and go on your way.

Jesus promises us there is more there if we want it. If you are lost in the dark, or if you are crying out to God for more, then it is my reverent prayer that this helps you take a step closer in your relationship with God. Jesus didn't intend to give you a new religion; He died so you could have a spiritual relationship directly with the Father.

I see people every day who are just going through the motions. They keep doing the same things over and over, getting more and more depressed because nothing changes. The beginning is opening your heart and inviting Jesus but that not all there is. That's the initial step. It is vital to build a two way relationship with the Holy Spirit. The purpose of the Holy Spirit is to provide a spiritual union with God.

A New Age of God

It is sad that there are so many people who feel God and the Bible are not necessary in their modern life and they are unaware of the vital need of the Holy Spirit in our lives and all the gifts that await us when we walk in alignment. Now most people believe the Holy Spirit is only in the Bible, something for biblical times and does not apply to our lives these days. The Holy Spirit is essential to your life for a deeper, spiritual love relationship with God. The Holy Spirit is your line of communication with the Almighty.

Generations have been taught that it is only the clergy and church leaders that had to have a constant relationship with God, but in fact it is the intention of God that each individual operate in spirit every day of their lives. The world is craving the relationship they were predestined to have; what they were created to have.

If you feel there should be more to your life, that's because there should be. There is more to you than you ever dreamed. You have been specifically designed to work coexist with the Holy Spirit. God put in place spiritual laws and principals in which He wants us to follow. Every kingdom has a King and every kingdom has laws and regulations. Society cannot function without laws of behavior and morals; the same is true with the kingdom of God.

Everyone is divinely designed to be united with the Holy Spirit so we all can operate at the Spiritual level we were originally created to have. This is the life of connectedness where you can function in joy.

We are in the midst a new age of God that is growing stronger and stronger. This is written to all of Gods children who are seeking answers or are just looking for more out of their life. You may not realize you are seeking God but you are striving for His presence and guidance; you just know you are seeking something to bring more

A New Age of God

meaning into your life. People are looking for guidance from psychics to guide them in their lives. What seekers need to realize is the guide they seek lives within. The only guide you need is the Holy Spirit residing within you.

We are experiencing a quickening (awakening) of the spirit that is growing stronger and stronger; calling the seekers home. If you have had visions or premonitions or have had prophetic dreams God is attempting to get your attention. You are being called by Holy Spirit for a purpose. He wants you to come home to the relationship you were predestined to have.

To the lost it is manifesting as a quickening of the pain of aloneness. That is why so many people are lost in drugs and alcohol trying to fill the gaping hole in their lives. If you are in despair or if you are feeling as if your life has lost its meaning, that is the Holy Spirit is trying to call you back into relationship. God will keep knocking at your door until you decide to accept Jesus so you may understand your purpose, accept His love and receive Him into your life. Why should you live in misery when there is peace and love awaiting you?

2012 has been prophesized as the end of the world. It is the death of an old era and the beginning of a new era. This quickening is causing a change in man's mindset and is stirring of Spirit of mankind. The Lord is reaching out to His people, stirring the spirit so we may awaken and begin the new age of awareness. Mankind has been slipping farther and farther from God and falling into the darkness of the carnal world for generations. It is time to prepare you so an educated decision can be made to change the way we see the world and make a stand and choose how we want our lives to be.

It is up to you to change your world and the world around you. If you can change your conception of the world by changing how you think you can change your universe.

A New Age of God

How you see yourself dictates how the world sees you. How you think decides how you see yourself.

You could live an androgynous life of political correctness; eliminate crosses and any signs of God from the Earth. You could let other people decide what we can do in our homes and how you must live your life or you can stand up for our right to believe and worship where and how you want. Do you want freedom of worship or do you want to just go along with the puppet masters that are trying to take away our rights? There is a time coming when you will have to make a choice. When the day comes I hope you will be prepared for the challenges that will come your way.

A meditation vision

I was isolated in a dark room with only a spot light that beamed down on where I was standing. I could hear people speaking and moving around but I could only see the glaring light in my eyes.

My husband and family had been taken away. I was in handcuffs and a man began interrogating me yelling at me about my terrorist ideals. He said I was a prisoner of the state and under the laws against terrorism I no longer had any rights or legal privileges and he had the power to decide what happened to me. I could not understand what I had done wrong. I was accused of holding antigovernment meetings at my home and business. My business was a non-profit group that helped the hungry and homeless and the meetings in my home were Bible studies. He said I was against the state policies and my subversive activities had to come to an end. It was the government's decision to decide the fate of the people.

A New Age of God

I had a choice either speak out publicly that I had been misled by subversive propaganda and had been brainwashed by a cult and they were there to rescue me. I needed to prove myself to the state by renouncing my faith and giving them the names of my co-conspirators. The cult was my church which had not been licensed and sanctioned by the state and the co-conspirators were the people who worked and worshipped with me.

I refused and was hauled outside to a truck that was full of other people. Late that night when the truck stopped and we were unloaded and marched to an enclosure surrounded with razor wire with search lights scanning the area. As the lights swept the compound all I could see were hundreds of people standing shoulder to shoulder. They did not show fear just stood defiant together as a brotherhood waiting to welcome the newest detainees.

God then spoke to me and said that this was a possible vision of the future that will happen if we do not change the way we see what is really happening in the world. We must open our eyes and see the truth. Other religions are being manipulated to destroy the Christian people and when we are gone then they will eliminate all religions and place a false religion and a false messiah on the throne to rule over us. It was my duty to relate my vision to help awake the seekers and doubters to help fight this movement that has already in begun.

Since that vision I have found out there is a panel of rich and powerful people who have a plan underway today to manipulate the world through the financial markets and big business to pull us away from a society of faith and make this an androgynous world. They have taken the basic necessities of life such as food, cotton, and oil into commercially traded commodities so they can manipulate the markets. Soon you will have to choose between

A New Age of God

buying gasoline and feeding your family. This is not an accident; it has been planned for a long time.

Once they control the basic necessities of life then they will set up an empty religion and a world economy that will lead the lost and the blind away from God and into following a false leadership using superstitions and fear to manipulate the masses.

What will you do when they come up to you and tell you that if you do not revoke your faith in Christ and join or you will not have a job or you might even go to prison? You won't be able to own a home or go to church and you will be ostracized for your antisocial behavior and you will not be allowed to be with your family or your friends because of your beliefs. How will you answer? Will you stand for God or fall alone?

Their greatest weapon will be self-righteousness and prejudice to dishonor us by showing our hypocrisies. We must strive to eliminate those weaknesses before they become weapons to be used against us.

You might say this could never happen but you must be prepared in faith for whatever trial comes before you so you will be able to discern what is really happening in the world around you. The world is already losing its mind and God is trying to wake you up so you can be prepared mentally and spiritually for the challenges that are upon us.

> **St. Matthew 7:7-9.** *Ask, and it shall be given; seek and you shall find; knock and it shall be opened for you: For every one that asks, receives; and he that seeks finds; and to him that knocks it shall be opened.*

The second key to oneness is obedience.

There comes a time when you must submit to the will of God and live in the manner you were designed to live. If you have been living a life of separation; how it that working out for you? Ask yourself if Jesus comes with the sunrise will you be ready to face God? If you die before you wake where will you go? Have you done all that you could in this life to be prepared? Life is not a bumper sticker slogan that says he that dies with the most toys win. Life well lived is one that does the best works is the winner.

There are millions of people who love the teachings of Jesus but have been hurt and disappointed for so long by religious dogma and law; I want the world to know that you can know God without all the structure and law that has left you cold. I am not saying you do not need a church family or that you do not need to follow the commandments of God but there is a way to honor God and live a spiritually focused life without just being a pew sitter in a church or trying to walk alone.

God is calling us to do away with the old dogma, throw out all the manmade idols, and the way we worship and grow into a new interactive relationship through love, devotion and connecting with the Holy Spirit. Something wonderful is coming and we will be in the middle of the revolution to the Jesus Way of life. We cannot know the time but we can recognize the season.

The gifts of the Holy Spirit are intended for every person that receives through Christ his new life in God. The church that Jesus preached for was a church of compassion and love. He came to bring people into a relationship that focused on brotherhood and forgiveness. Through His sacrifice, death and resurrection He had

A New Age of God

made possible for the Holy Spirit to be present on the Earth for each and every one of us.

Jesus' life was to be the beginning of a new age of miracles and transformation and in the beginning it was but man being man, he had to take the word and build a church full of rules and regulations that has altered and manipulated what Jesus intended. The Gnostics took the rational mind to design the church into their preconceived image.

Jesus wanted us to have the ability to directly receive direction from the Holy Spirit and this would have taken the power and authority from the priests. This has been made available to all mankind through Jesus and His teachings which explains why these teachings were suppressed. If we have the ability to directly access the Holy Spirit and have to power to each of us do the works of God then where does that leave the priesthood? The priests of old felt the ordinary man was too carnal and ignorant to understand the ways of God and it was their responsibility to guide and protect mankind. The rationalized they were guiding the uneducated to prevent him from being confused.

Jesus said that we are to create a world here as it is in Heaven. Our daily bread is the word of God and our compass throughout our day is the Holy Spirit.

The old church of religion consisted of promises of a God filled life but they do not tell you what you should be doing to nurture and grow our faith are not being put forth in the church today; what you get is a copy of a prepared sermon and you read along. They have structured todays church so there is no room for the Holy Spirit to interact with the Pastor and the congregation and then they wonder why they don't feel God. Everything is on a set schedule according to a formula; perfectly organized to get you out for lunch.

A New Age of God

Most people feel like they have been judged as soon as they walk through the door of the church, before you say a word you have been assessed by your appearance. Remember you are seeking Gods approval and no one else. Our Lord and Savior is a come as you are God and He has reserved the job of judgment for Himself. We have to reach out to the least if we want to do the most for Him.

Christians have a responsibility to be the Earthly representatives of Christ. We are to be the body of Christ and we all must follow in His footsteps, doing His work and spreading His word. I have great news, you can come to know God and find that joy that you have been searching for. You can develop that loving heart you were meant to possess.

The third key is oneness of intent.

It is absolutely essential you live your life with intent. Simply put living with intent is making up your mind and following through with your plan. You must have a plan on how to live your life and see it clearly. You cannot live as your emotions dictate at any given moment. You have to live with your intent regardless of how you feel. God will help you to align those emotions and help you build the life you intend to have.

You cannot live a life without intent or you will only wander in the dark with no purpose. An intentional brings you a true purpose of life into focus. People all over the world are wasting their lives trying to fill that void with sex, drugs and alcohol. They have turned to new age gurus that teach self-empowerment, meditation and the basic science of God but they have omitted the love relationship that true worship can bring.

A New Age of God

I don't care if you go to church every Sunday; if you aren't moving closer to God then you are just pew sitting! If every day you are not moving closer to God then you are stagnating. Lip service is not what God is after, He wants praise and worship, and He wants to be a part of your life on Saturday night as well as Sunday morning. I am talking about a way of life, a new way of thinking about your life and a new way to wake up to a new world every morning. To live in peace within and to create the life you want.

You must live your life with intent. This means you have to know what you want and have a plan how to get it. If your intent is to be closer to God and live a spiritual life then you need to know what you need to do. If you want to help a certain group of people then decide how to do it and make a plan. If you live without intent then you are sailing your boat without a rudder and leaving it up to the tides and the wind to guide you.

Everything you do must have an intent, such as why are you reading this or what do you plan to get from reading this. Life is full of questions and it is up to you to find the answers. I have two intentions with this book; the first is to get you to think for yourself about your life and family. The second intent is to give you a structured approach to getting closer to God and enhancing your life with God's guidance.

The fourth key to oneness is commitment.

In any relationship there will come a time where you have to put up or shut up! You have to decide if you want to make a commitment to the relationship. If you commit to Christ your life can be an awesome miracle. You can have peace; joy and security of knowing you are joined in the

A New Age of God

family of Christ who gives salvation to all who dedicate their life.

You can be forgiven for anything; you can have a new life. Committing to Christ is the beginning of the greatest relationship you can ever have. Nothing can come before Him in your life, but when He resides in your heart your capacity to love others grows to limitless proportions. You will have a deeper relationship in all areas of your life. You will see the world with new eyes.

The Love of the King

The King wants to come into your heart
You must tear down your idols
Be single-minded in faith
Why is it so hard to express your faith in God?
Why is it so easy to put your faith in the things of man?
Man fluctuates like the wind
Driven by the flow of his emotions
The feet of man is made of clay
With a little wind and water the clay begins to erode
In times of drought clay cracks and breaks apart
Clay on its own cannot stand the test of time
Under the hands of the Potter the clay may be reshaped
Made into a thing of beauty
Properly treated and tempered
Glazed it can last a hundred years
Rely on the Potter to prepare your feet of clay
Glaze yourself in God's grace
Through faith and believing all things are possible
God is your protector; your armor

Every prayer brings you on one step closer
Every day HE is there to protect and guide you
Take out your armor and put it on

A New Age of God

Cast out all who come against you

Rebuke those who impede your progress

When you let HIM be your KING

Your anointing will come

So what are you willing to do? Are you up to take a step out in faith?

Never ever believe you are beyond redemption. Whoever you are, whatever you have done, you are loved. Whenever a child becomes lost their family does not stop loving their child. If anything their love becomes more acute because of the separation, loss and worry.

The same is true for God. He wants you to find your way home. Jesus is calling you home to His unconditional love and forgiveness. Allow the Father to guide His priceless child home. It is not called salvation for nothing! Grace can be yours, the past can be washed clean and you too can become a new person in Christ. Let Jesus rename you just as Saul the persecutor became Paul the Apostle. You can rise from your knees and shine in His glory!

CHAPTER 3

Foundation

Acts 20:32. *And now, brethren I commend you to God, and to the word of His grace, which is able to build you up, and to give you an inheritance among all them which are sanctified.*

Every day people spend their days just going through the motions. The majority of the people are walking around hypnotized by the world. The definition of insanity is doing the same thing over and over and expecting a different result; yet people keep living their lives just that way, getting more depressed and discouraged because they never see any improvement in their lives.

Some people say all you need to do is dedicate yourself to Jesus and that's all there is to changing your life. Don't misunderstand me, that is the crucial moment in your Spiritual life; it can be the beginning of more works and wonders in your future.

There awaits a deeper, more personal love relationship with God that will give you the tools to discover your life work. Any relationship requires work and as with all

A New Age of God

matters of love you have to give it away to receive. You need to work on giving love in all facets of your life. Leave your judgments and criticisms to God. It is Gods job to judge, the Holy Spirit to convict and Jesus sits on the Mercy seat to provide salvation to all who seek Him.

You know there is more to life than what you see every day and there is more than you ever dreamed. Every human being has been divinely designed specifically to lead a dual life. Even though we live in a physical body, we are made to have an intimate connection with the Holy Spirit; we are blessed to walk on the Earth while being guided through life by the Holy Spirit. This is the level where we attain the joy and creativeness God intended for us.

> **John 5:23-24.** *That all men should I honor the Son, even as they honor the Father. He that honors not the Son honors not the Father that has sent Him. Verily, verily I say onto you, he that hears my word and believe on Him that sent me, hath everlasting life, and shall not come into condemnation; but is passed from death unto life.*

The new age of God has begun and it's growing stronger and stronger. There is a message coming through to all God's children through dreams and visions, which speak of things coming to pass and things to be done.

There are people who are dedicating themselves to help guide all those who feel the urging of the Holy Spirit and are seeking answers. You may be being urged to action even though you may not realize you are being called by God and that you are striving for His presence and guidance.

A New Age of God

The new age movement has been a strong attraction to people who want a spiritual life without religion, rules and regulations. They have blended eastern philosophy with Christianity, to find a connection with the Father while ignoring the spiritual laws of God or accepting the Divinity of Jesus. This explains why people spend thousands of dollars on physics and guru's trying to find the guidance that they need from the Holy Spirit. The New Age movement seeks to achieve a spiritual life without all the window dressing of rules and regulations of God. The problem with the New Age position is much like the Universalist philosophy, which believes since God loves everyone there are no commandments on how to live. They believe everyone goes to Heaven to wait for their next incarnation to give it another shot.

If you love Jesus but the dogma of religion leaves you cold, then you are not alone millions of people feel abandoned and betrayed by religion. The spirit of self-righteousness has done immeasurable damage to Gods children.

The ultra-conservative evangelical movement has isolated themselves and caused a shadow to fall on the Christian Church around the world. You can have God without all the law and judgment that religion has placed between you and God. You can come as you are to God and He will welcome you home.

If you want to feel power of love in your life you must concentrate upon changing the focus of your life. All that you see as truth will change as you learn to create your life through Christ. What you have seen as life in the flesh is really death to the Spirit. When you find life in Christ you will see the joy of the universe open up to you.

1 Thessalonians 5:15-19. *See that none render evil for evil unto any man; but ever follow that*

> *which is good, both among yourselves, and to all men. Rejoice evermore! Pray without ceasing. In everything give thanks: for this is the will of God in Christ Jesus concerning you. Quench not the Spirit.*

Each prayer brings you closer to God, each time you meditate on your Spiritual connection you bring yourself closer to walking in the Spirit realm with the Holy Spirit. Every time you read the word of GOD aloud you increase your faith. Each time you praise and worship you come into the direct attention of the Father. Just as a child raises their hands up to their Father for attention and help, that is how you should reach up to God. Let the Lord know how you feel and sing out HIS praises. This is the heart of opening up the direct intimacy between you and God.

To Love God

To love God is to love everyone

To love God is to be one with your God

To be one with God is to see love in all things

To be one with God is to see the miracle of all His creation

Money and religious dogma are at the root of the dissention in the world. Self-righteousness of religion has blinded the masses so they cannot accept each other's choices on what is the truth. Every human being must be allowed to make their own choices and make their own mistakes.

Coveting all things that glitter will make you miss the gold in your life. People of God do not live for things; affluence and comfort are something that God wants you to have but as a side benefit of His favor. You can own things but things should not own you. People of God want a peace which comes with the Lord brings to you that cannot be bought with things. When you live a God centered life the affluence of the King will become yours as a side benefit as long as you don't feel it is wrong to be successful in life. You do not have to live a martyred life of poverty and depravation to live a Godly life.

The enemy uses the ego to spur the desire for temporary things. Worship the body and it will wither from age; worship your things and they will lose their luster and be taken from you. Worship money and it will slip between your fingers. You will lose all things you put before God, until you learn what is truly the greatest treasure of you existence...God's love.

The King is coming

What if Jesus comes with the sunrise?

Will you be ready to face Him?

It's time to tear down you idols...whatever they may be

Take out your spiritual armor and put it on

Cast away all who go against you

Accept Him as your King

Your blessings will come

He won't make you change

The choice is yours

He is waiting on you to move

He wants to take you to the next level in the kingdom!

Hebrews 11:1. *Now faith is the substance of things hoped for, the evidence of things not seen.*

Hebrews 11:3. *Through faith we understand that the worlds were framed by the word of God, so that things which are seen were not made of things which do appear.*

Luke 17:6. *If you have the faith as a grain of mustard seed, you might say unto this sycamine tree, be you plucked up by the root and be you planted in the sea; and it should obey you.*

Faith and the word

Faith is operating in the word. It is a fact, something you believe just as surely as the ground under your feet and the sky above you. Faith is ever present in the now, not something that might happen tomorrow. Faith is manifested in the God realm and not on this side. You are what you believe and you cannot please anyone without faith especially God.

Faith is something you grow. Faith comes by hearing the word of God which plants the seed of truth. Faith grows from your reading the Bible aloud every day. You cannot find God through intellect, only by faith through hearing the word of God. Speak your faith regularly even if in the beginning you don't believe what you are saying. When I started this process I felt like a phony saying what I did not completely feel or understand, but what I felt had nothing to do with it. My conscious mind was uncomfortable with what I was beginning and constantly

A New Age of God

urged me to go back to my old routine. I had to constantly remind myself what I was working on achieving.

> **Hebrews 11:6.** *But without faith it is impossible to please Him; for He that comes to God must believe that He is, and that He is a rewarder of them that diligently seek Him.*

My mind cannot decide my faith or understand the ways and means of God. My emotions do not dictate my faith, or the decisions I make in my life because emotion is a product of the logical mind and the goal of the mind is to keep you where you have always been. The human being is a creature of habit that is led by the mind.

You must start to have faith in something that God provides, whether it is in His mercy or it is His power to heal; start with something you believe in because faith grows faith. My faith grows through the heart and the spirit.

Faith comes from sincere prayer. Pray with your heart for your relationship with God to grow and have belief and your relationship to God will grow. Believe what you pray for is already created. Have a clear vision of what you want to receive, see it, feel it and know your prayer has manifested.

This is the way Jesus operated and He wants you to function the same way! The power of The I Am is at your command; the power of I AM will give you the authority and dominion to manifest in your life. You are an extension of Almighty God. You are in training for reigning on Earth. God never responds for anything but through faith. If you pray in faith, you pray in believing. If you allow fear and worry to creep in fear will destroy you petition and annul your faith. If you have faith in

A New Age of God

the sunrise, you do not lay there worrying about the sun because you know the sun will rise tomorrow and that is how faith must work in your prayers.

Pray in faith then give thanks unto the Lord and stop searching with your head. When the prayer goes up with fervor and favor will flow. When a child believes, they don't go through a debate of the possibilities or the pro and cons; there is no doubt, they get so excited with the anticipation for what they know will happen. That should be the desire and excitement in your heart to please God. Blessings will follow unlimited and unhindered and it will all come to pass. Never ever rely on other peoples anointing to sustain you. You are made to stand alone in faith.

You are the reason for the universe! God gave man dominion on the Earth, so you have control; you must stand up for yourself, show your authority and walk without fear and your faith will cause God to reach out to you and answer your petition. If you are obedient in the dictates of God and you operate in prayer and faith, you will reap the fat of the land. God will favor you in all aspects of your life. You will walk in abundance in all things. There are far greater things in store for you than you can imagine. Believe you are the instrument of God's work.

God is a rewarder to those who diligently seek him. When you sincerely work in worship of the Lord you build a relationship; as in all true love relationships the more love you give the more you receive. The more you focus your love on the Lord the stronger your faith will become. The stronger your faith becomes the more you manifest in your life which grows your faith. Each prayer forges a golden link in a chain of faith between you and God which allows you to walk stronger and farther in your spirit life.

The Prayer Closet

You need a place that you can call your own for prayer, meditation and praise. You need to build an atmosphere of love and reverence. This needs to be a sacred place that is reserved for God. This is where you can be alone with God. You need to read the word aloud, play inspiring music, pray and praise out loud and meditate on the Lord.

It doesn't have to be a separate room or anything elaborate; you just need a corner for solitude. The most important thing is that this place remains sacred to you and you respect that holiness at all times. You will start feel God's presence when you enter your worship place. You will build a spiritual agape over time that will become your portal into your God zone. That is where I pray, meditate, praise and where I do all my writing. If I am to write on behalf of the Lord I must work within His atmosphere.

Think of it as building a reverential atmosphere. Once you have an environment that speaks to you then you develop an atmosphere. This atmosphere is something invisible that surrounds us and that inspires us to do great things. This will become your place for private worship and you will begin to notice the change that comes over you when you go to your private space. You must keep the atmosphere stirred and see your vision clearly. More and more you will begin to sense the presence of the Holy Spirit as you grow closer to God. It is essential you expect this to be a holy place and respect this space because you will receive what you believe.

Soon you will start to manifest your vision and blessings will follow unlimited and unhindered. It is an awesome feeling when you start to operate in favor with the Lord. You will walk with the Holy Spirit every day and know He is with you and He will be there to guide you every step of the way.

A New Age of God

In times past, a home had chapels or alters for the family to worship at. Even the poorest people had some sort of space for worship as an integral part of their homes. This is no longer even considered when planning a home. It is time for attitudes to change so faith can become central in the family. You must have a sacred space set aside to help you keep your faith uppermost in your life if you want to have a more intimate relationship with God.

Think of it as if the Lord residing within a huge mansion and only those who find favor are allowed into the inner recesses. As you begin to feel your connection growing, you will notice how strong the feeling of love will grow within you. It is possible to move farther and farther into the realm of God and be granted more and access to his favor and be taken farther and farther into the kingdom. Once you start to gain the favor of the King more and more of his grace and favor will start to fall into your life.

To live in grace is the goal of every worshipper. Living in grace is like living in a peaceful ease where you know you are loved and all you need is being provided. There is a flow to your life that fits together like a perfect picture. I compare the feeling of grace like floating slowly down a lazy river on a perfect day with a warm sun shining down and a gentle breeze caressing my skin; without a care or thought perfectly at peace.

This is the feeling I have when I am meditating on oneness with God. I get overwhelmed with a feeling of love that fills me to overflowing. I know that the presence of God is with me and it makes wish I were a poet. I wish I could write Psalms of devotion to God the way David did. My heart sings Psalms to Him but there are no words to express the song.

> **Psalm 77:12.** *I will meditate also of all your work and talk of your doings.*

A New Age of God

I strongly urge you to start meditating daily and work on learning to focus on God. In the beginning start with a five or ten minute meditation and gradually lengthen the time as you become more comfortable with the process. Most people find it very hard to clear your mind and focus. Your mind will fight you and you will have to bring your mind back to your purpose. Find some inspirational music or the sounds of nature to help establish the mood.

The first thing you must do is pray for guidance and protection. Pray for the Lord to guide closer and closer to oneness, that He will surround you with HIS love and protection. Declare your intention and your love. Close your eyes and focus on your breathing and get as comfortable and relaxed as you can. Make yourself a mantra such as Lord I seek to move closer to you or anything that describes your goal. Repeat this over and over to yourself. If your mind wanders just refocus your mind; slow down your breathing, relax your body, and clear your mind. As time goes by it will get easier and easier to maintain your focus.

You can also do what I call a rolling meditation; this is just pondering a subject over and over such as something or someone you want to understand or something you want to receive. Any spare time in your day just roll the question or phrase over and over again. This is not as beneficial to the body as an actual meditation but it helps to form the habit of having an ongoing conversation with God.

What color do you associate with the light of God? As you are meditating visualize that color flowing down upon you, if you need healing visualize a color you associate with healing and see and feel the light of God penetrating your very being. The more real you make it, the more senses you include, the more connection you will have. As you are visualizing the direct the light to the area that need healing and feel the warming heat of God working on your body.

Once you get more proficient start allowing a breath between each statement. The universe rests in the breaths between the words, in the brief silence between the thoughts. The silent pauses will gradually become longer and longer as the peace continues to grow. You will begin to receive inspirations, ideas or flashes of pictures that relate to your needs. They may not make sense, but that is your logical mind trying to rationalize. You are bypassing the physical and are reaching into the temporal zone of the Almighty.

There are many side benefits to meditating, your stress level drops, and it lowers your blood pressure and makes you a much calmer person. The universe helps put things in perspective. Things that used to worry you will begin to dissipate and you will see with new eyes.

Faith is a knowing that is based on belief. If you believe then you know; there should not be a question mark at the end of faith or belief. .

> **John 12:44.** *That they all be as you, Father, art in Me, and I in You, that they also may be one in US; that the world believe that You have sent me.*

You must believe in the power of Jesus Christ.

Jesus was born with a purpose, to show the world He is the Son of God and that the Father resides in Him. He prepared for his mission for thirty years and taught for three years. There was a presence in Him that could be felt as he passed, the very presence of God emanated from

A New Age of God

his being. He knew your heart when he looked at you. Jesus changed lives just by passing by. Healing by word, touch or even by thought; He brought forth the power of God wherever he went.

Jesus didn't go to funerals; He raised the dead. He taught peace, compassion and love. The Geneva Convention is based on the principals of Jesus philosophy. He wanted people to look within and judge themselves before they were to judge others; teaching you should look inside first before you cast stones.

Jesus taught forgiveness and change in a time persecution was the rule of the day. He loved his enemies to the point He took Saul, a persecutor and murderer of Christians and changed him into Paul, one of the greatest Apostles that wrote the majority of the New Testament. There is nothing that cannot be changed through the love of God touching your heart. You can be healed of anything, and through God all things are possible.

Most people say Jesus died for our sins but do not comprehend what that truly means. There is a meditation exercise on compassion where you are asked to focus on Jesus' life and to imagine all He suffered and take in all the suffering and injustice in the world and experience all the pain that is going on in the world. You are to hold onto all that pain and suffering as long as you can stand it and then release it to God and see God receiving it all. The feeling upon release is supposed to be as close to peace as man can visualize or experience.

I would like you to do a similar exercise but place yourself in Jesus' shoes. I want you to take the walk to Calvary and place yourself on the cross. You are being publicly humiliated by the people who were singing your praises a few days ago. Being dragged from one judge to another while being ridiculed, cursed and spat upon, flogged in public with whips with hooks attached till the flesh was

A New Age of God

torn from your back, sides and stomach; your beard is ripped from His face and you are ripped and torn beyond recognition, then you are given your cross to carry up to Calvary. You are wearing a crown of thorns that are pressing into the bones of your head. Your blood is running into your eyes, you fall to the ground in exhaustion and you are forced to lift your cross and go on.

Once there you are laid down on the cross and 6 inch spikes are driven into your wrists; your feet are overlapped and an 8 inch spike is driven through the arches of your feet, impaling them together, then you are lifted up into the air and planted into the ground. The gravity begins pulling at the spikes tearing the tendons in your wrist that attaches to the shoulder. Your blood is running into your eyes and down your back, down your legs pooling on the ground. To breathe you must use your back muscles because the tendons of your arms are useless. Your back cannot support you for long so you must try to use your feet to support you. The agony is so bad you must alternate back and forth to stay alive. Jesus endured this agony for over three hours!

The body has completely bled out and only water is pouring from your body and in a few minutes more you pass away. They are worried you will not die before sundown so they drive a spear in your side to make sure you are really dead and to help the process along. The physical agony is bad enough but you are literally suffering the sins of mankind, voluntarily taking on the wounds of the world along with your own physical pain while hanging there. Understand He not only suffered His own physical pain but He also took on the pain of the world so that you and I could have access to the Holy Spirit and that He could intercede for your mercy. He loved you that much; He suffered beyond belief for you because He loves you and He believes in you.

A New Age of God

The blood of the Lamb had to be shed to fulfill the biblical prophecy of the Messiah. When it could not get any worse God pulled His contact with Jesus and left Him alone hanging on the cross so He would feel the torment of the lost who did not know God. That is why Jesus cried out asking why the Father had forsaken Him. I ask you to allow yourself to attempt this and experience what Jesus did for you on that day.

You need to consciously receive what was done for you so you can decide what you will do with that gift. I tried but I didn't last very long. I wound up in the fetal position sobbing asking the Lord to forgive me for not being stronger, for not being a better person for Him. No mere human being could have voluntarily allowed this.

Before our time God knew His children needed a Messiah to go down to the Earth and show His children the Way and the Light. Someone needed to teach and lead His people; to suffer the sins of the world and be resurrected to show the world there is a living God and that death is not the end of life but a transition to the beginning of an eternal life. His sacrifice tore the veil of separation that was placed between God and man when Adam defied God in the garden.

Jesus knew the consequences and He knew the ignorance of mankind but He was willing to do anything for His Father and Jesus loved us so much He would endure anything if it saved just one person.

Today the world is in desperate need of an Army of believers to take up their armor and stand for His principles and His work. People who are willing to do anything God will for the good of the kingdom. You need to be prepared to go to spiritual war to defend this life in Christ. I am standing here within my covenant with the Father to live and work for Him to the death if necessary

A New Age of God

and I am asking you to join me and stand for Christ before it is too late for the world.

Put on your spiritual armor, stand in His righteousness, pick up your sword and approach the throne of God. Lay your sword at the Lords feet, humble yourself before the Father of us all and commit your sword to His work. Make a covenant with God to do his works, to walk in faith and follow his light throughout your existence.

Putting your faith in God isn't a gamble; the love of God for His children is absolute. He doesn't waver or go back on His word. He wants you to make a covenant with Him. People have made history with their faith in themselves. What could they have done with the help of God? Trust in Jesus, He is a limitless God! Refuse to accept or place limits in your life. God wants you to be the best and have the best so believe in the temple of yourself. Through Christ you can do all things. Believe in the unachievable, do not listen to the world, and do not be distracted by the world. Do not be transformed by the world but be transformed by faith and by the word and you can transform your world.

Create your own world, build your own environment that will be the unseen by the world but it will exist as surely as the clothes you wear. Faith will dissolve the distance between you and God. If you keep showing up for your appointed time with God and you keep your eyes on God you will see a new world appear that will replace the old one. Every prayer, each time you praise you increase your faith and the love you send out. People will begin to sense a new atmosphere around you; strangers will begin to react differently when they meet you. Children and animals will be drawn to you just to get a little of the God that surrounds you.

I think of my life now being in Technicolor instead of black and white. I am living a life of Technicolor joy! Faith

A New Age of God

believes beyond the unseen world and creates in Heaven what you will receive on Earth. Your possibilities are limitless if you keep your eyes on God because our God is a God of life.

A word of caution: Be careful when you read the word of God, we all have a tendency to color what we read by our background and what we have been taught. Read the Bible as if was a newspaper giving you the news of the day and let the Holy Spirit interpret the good news to your heart and you will be given what you need. Anytime you are going to read the Word, say a short prayer for inspiration and guidance. It will make all the difference in the word in your understanding.

In the beginning the word of God will not speak to you but as you build your relationship with the Holy Spirit you will begin to see new relevance surface. The Bible will start to speak to you in clearer and clearer messages. Every story in the Bible is designed to teach and the message sometimes exists between the lines. I can read a chapter five times and still receive something new when I am looking for guidance.

You need to have a plan on how you want to live your life and what you want to do. You need a clear vision of where you want to go. Visualize final result you want clearly as if it you are drawing a portrait. The clearer the vision the easier it is to manifest. It needs to become an obsession that you are willing to devote yourself to receiving. Then you can get an idea for how you want to achieve your goal and what steps you need to take to achieve it. Have a plan and work your plan. See what you want to accomplish and work backwards to see what you need to do. You must see clearly, have a plan and work the plan each and every day.

The things you need to succeed will come to you and the people will become available that you need to surround yourself with to succeed in manifesting your vision. You

A New Age of God

will build a team that sees clearly your vision so you can work your plan. It is your responsibility to make them see your vision. Once the vision and the plan becomes clear and you all start working in like mind things will start to help you get your group working together.

There is a great power in a group of people who share in a vision and a belief. People of like precious faith are the most dramatic groups of workers. Your vision will cause you to have to move out of your comfort zone and grow in confidence and faith. You provide the clear vision and God will fill in the details. If you work from confidence and faith you are limitless and it won't be long until you will have to dream bigger dreams and have new visions. You must have a plan and you must work the plan!

God does not reward those who just sit and wish; you must be willing to work and he will give you the tools and the materials. Seeing the end result will give you a new beginning. Keep showing up and keep working in faith and the world will be yours. You will be a supernatural wonder because you are working in the supernatural to create in the natural.

If you have had dreams of who you are that is different from who you are today I urge you to take those dreams seriously. I have had dreams of doing things that were absurd at the time but they were prophetic to prepare me.

Joseph is a perfect example of manifesting a dream in the Book of Genesis. Joseph knew who he was from the time he was a small child. He was the most loved of his brothers and they were jealous of him. Joseph had dreams at night of being a King and he would relate those dreams to his brothers. Satan saw the power and faith of Joseph and set out to ruin him so Satan entered into his brother's hearts and inflamed their self-righteousness anger to the point they sold him into slavery and told his father he had been killed.

A New Age of God

Joseph wound up as a slave in Egypt but he held on to his vision of being a King. He quickly rose to the head of his master's household and even the wife of the master had to come to Joseph if she wanted something. He carried himself as a king even when he was a slave and the wife of the master was jealous of Joseph's position with her husband falsely accused Joseph of trying to seduce her and the Master put Joseph in prison.

While he was in prison his master started have troubling dreams that no one could interpret for him and finally out of desperation he sent for Joseph. Joseph interpreted the dreams and discerned Egypt would have years of prosperity followed by years of famine. Joseph devised a plan to store up food so the people of Egypt would not suffer during the famine.

When the famine came Joseph's family was suffering and Joseph's father hearing that there was food in Egypt sent all but his youngest son to Egypt to buy food. Joseph recognized his brothers but they failed to recognize him.

In the end they had to bow down to Joseph just as he had envisioned and they had to go to their father and admit what they had done. So even though they tore Joseph from his family, Joseph held onto his dreams and regardless of the situation through God he manifested his dream and got his family back. Joseph never lost his vision of himself and his faith in God never wavered.

You too must keep your vision of who you are. God works in the realm of the eternal where time does not exist; everything in Heaven is already created and exists in the now. We have to overcome the ignorance of time and accept that the eternal is more real than this existence. Everything you need exists in the invisible world of God and all we have to do is reach up into the eternal realm beyond time and bind what we want. To succeed you must claim it and accept God's will in your work. You cannot receive beyond your mental capacity and you cannot manifest what you cannot see clearly. You must understand what you want, see it clearly and believe that you will receive.

Jesus taught and works in the supernatural realm of the Father so you must elevate your problem to the supernatural realm of God for a solution.

> **John 1:2.** *In the beginning was the Word, and the Word was with God, and the word was God.*

God needs you to give the word voice for it to manifest. We have been given the unique authority to create with our words that which is already created in heaven. All things already exist in Heaven and then we bind them we bind them on earth from Heaven as our own. First it is Gods, and then it can be created by you. Understand you are manifesting from the God realm and time is nonexistent in the eternal.

Time is a creation of man that began when Adam fell from Grace and the veil of separation was created. Time is the illusion of the enemy to keep you tied in bondage. The world is Satan's realm and he wants you kept in limitation by time to keep you in dominion. Time exists only in this realm; Faith is above time from the spirit realm. Faith is operating on the word.

You are rich beyond the imagination.

The enemy wants you to believe you are powerless and limited. Jesus operated in the spiritual realm and manifested all from the Father. Jesus spoke and manifested in the spiritual realm which operates out of

A New Age of God

time and it is evidenced when He manifested a gold coin in a fish's mouth, when He killed a barren fig tree and when He resurrected the dead to give a few examples.

So when you speak and call forth from the Father in Jesus' name you need to see clearly what you want, speak out of time and look into the spiritual realm for your creation. You must manifest with faith and expectation if you are to receive.

God has given this power to man and that is why what you think, feels, and act matters. You are who you believe you and that is a product of your thoughts and emotions. We are the only species that was created to be reprogrammable. That means it is possible to reprogram all the inner turmoil, negativity and find peace and happiness. It is possible to reinvent yourself, just as you can reeducate yourself for a new career.

A parrot might be able to mimic words, but it has no awareness of self or what it says; it only echoes what it hears and therefore cannot give thought to the word and create through its words. Man is the only one created to have the power. God designed man to be of God and gave them the capacity for a complete understanding of the works of God. Every day you may waver in your focus but you must keep pulling yourself back into alignment. Today more and more people in the world are seeking answers to the questions that they are not sure how to ask.

They need to understand how God works with them and through their words so they can manifest God's works. God has given man dominion over the Earth and for God's work to manifest His works. That is why God calls us to join Him to accomplish His will. God designed man to work with Him as one unit under His guidance.

The inheritance is yours whether you believe it or not. You are born of royal lineage from the Creator. This is a

A New Age of God

natural power and it will work for your best interest or you can misuse it and draw many negative things your way. When you say that is the way it has always been you are reinforcing the same occurrences over and over. You become a negative self-fulfilling prophecy.

Lord's Prayer

Our Father (the Father of us all) who are in Heaven,
Holy be your name,
Your kingdom come, (create the kingdom within)
Your will be done on Earth as it is in Heaven (bind on Earth what is already created in Heaven)
Give us this day, our daily bread (the word of God)
Forgive us out trespass (salvation)
As we forgive those who trespass against us (to be forgiven we must forgive and leave it in the past)
Lead us not into temptation (keep our eyes and hearts on Him)
And deliver us from evil (His law and His protection deliver us)
For yours is the kingdom (the spiritual kingdom within)
And the power (His power and it resides within)
And the glory (our praise of the Father)
Forever and ever (one life, one love, eternal)

People take the Lord's Prayer for granted and fail to realize the power that is embedded in the wording. It is an affirmation to God. For an affirmation to work you must understand its purpose. Within the prayer is the instruction for how life is to be lived and created. Our daily bread is not food but the word of God and His love. We have the power to manifest God's will down to Earth. All we need already exists in Heaven and all we have to do is bind it for ourselves in Jesus' name and call it forth in faith and claim it.

The reason there were so many miracles in the Old Testament is that the people listened to the prophets and they expected them to manifest. People were aware that they were subject to God's will and that He would

A New Age of God

move in their behalf. Prophets were revered as guides for their survival in following Gods will. We get what we expect, either for bad or for good. People today have no expectations from God so do not receive and use that as proof that He does not exist.

The word of God is written so that by a means we as humans can understand so we may know the Father. When you read the word for recreation you do not receive the true meaning within. When you read through study, in faith, each word becomes a part of a complete thought that becomes a communication in unity with God and He provides the inspiration that moves you into understanding of His word and His intent through the use of the mind.

Mark 4:14. *The Source sows the word.*

Whatever you say sows your world. The power of the word lies within each of us and what we say determines our future. If you sow negativity then you will attract negative things. The absolute worst thing you can do to your life is say there is nothing I can do about it because you are leaving yourself powerless. If you believe your life is a train wreck then it will be as you have spoken.

Psalm 102:16 *When the Lord shall bind up Zion (God's people); He shall appear in His glory.*

Your mind believes what your mouth says.

When you bind with the Lord you will begin to appear in your glory and your glory will be an affirmation of what

A New Age of God

God has created within. When you read His word aloud you allow the words to take root in the spirit and you comprehend in the mind through the ears. You mind believes what you say; your mind relies on you to provide the right thoughts information to guide you.

If you do not provide the proper information for your mind then you will wind up repeating the same thoughts and remain in your own old programming. We are living in a time of a curse based system and we are constantly limiting ourselves simply because we do not understand the universal laws. Society lives in a sea of deceit meant to reinforce the ways of the world and we have swallowed it hook line and sinker.

You must expect with the joy and anticipation like a young child at Christmas and you will begin to create miracles all around you. Whatever you expect, a healing, wisdom, or discernment it can be yours; you will create miracles. If you turn the door knob don't you expect to be able to open the door? It is that simple! It is an acquired knowing that you build within your life.

Just like that child at Christmas that is how we should create through our expectations.

Expectation coincides with your need to control your mind and your words. You have an effect on yourself and all those around you. You thoughts, attitude and purpose will profoundly affect all the people in your life. A little kindness and love go a long way. People want to feel loved and appreciated, I don't care what they do, and they want to be recognized for what they do.

To the same point if you have children, all you do, say and how you relate to them molds who they are. If you do not hold them in respect, how can they respect themselves? See you're potential and fulfill it, see their potential, find out where they want to go and lead them there. If you live a life of denial, separate from the spirit then your child will not benefit from the peace, love and harmony knowing you walk in the arms of God. You could be responsible for your child not living a God filled life. Do you want to face the Lord and explain why do did not teach your children about God and the miracles of His love?

> **2 Corinthians 4:2-4.** *We have renounced the hidden things of dishonesty, not walking in craftiness, nor handling the word of God deceitfully; but by the manifestation of truth commending ourselves to every man's conscience in the sight of God. But if our gospel be hid, it is to be hid to them that are lost. In whom the god of this world (Satan has the world) hath blinded the minds of them which believe not, lest the light of the glorious gospel of Christ, who is the image of God, should shine unto them.*

We create miracles every day.

With our hearts (faith), through our minds (belief) and they spring from our mouths (in His name & in His authority) and frame our world (manifestation).

The Lord said my people are being destroyed by ignorance! In the beginning the Trinity was God, the Word and the Holy Spirit; they were three but they were one according to the miracle of God that though all are separate in their works they are one in spirit.

A New Age of God

God knew man was lost and there was no one on earth that could bring the people back to Him so God took the word and made it flesh. God took the Word wrapped it in flesh and bone and implanted the Word into Mary and through His miraculous ability only the untarnished blood of God circulated in the child. And thus Jesus went from the spirit of the word to the word in the flesh.

> **John 1:1-4.** *In the beginning was the word, and the word was with God, and the word was God. The same was in the beginning with God. All things were made by Him; and without Him was not anything made that was made. And the Light shines in the darkness; and the darkness comprehended it not.*

Read the scripture above and where it speaks of the word replace Jesus' name and see if the meaning becomes clearer. It is stated in the Bible that Jesus was the word and the light. In the beginning was Jesus, and Jesus was with God, and Jesus was God. The Jesus was God in the beginning and is God today. Jesus is the Light that shines in the darkness and without Jesus you will not comprehend the things of God.

The Word was Jesus and Jesus was the Word. Jesus is the Word and the Light. The Trinity evolved into God, the Son and the Holy Spirit all separate but one. God used the word to frame the world and the word is as powerful on earth as it is heaven. We are commanded to frame our world through the dominion given unto us by God when He created us to walk the earth.

Jesus manifested from the Father and we manifest through the name of Jesus to the Father. The power lies within the name of Jesus.

A New Age of God

> **1 John 3:8.** *The wind blows where it will, and you hear the sound thereof, but cannot tell from where it comes, and where it goes: so is every one that is born of the spirit.*

You cannot understand where the direction of the Holy Spirit comes from when He speaks to you, it just happens and when you pray in spirit you do not know where the prayer is directed because it is mandated by the Holy Spirit to achieve a purpose that only God knows. You will just be an instrument to perform His work, because God needs you to give voice to His word for Him to manifest the change He desires.

You must claim (declare) your inheritance as royal blood, claim what you are praying for, and call it into being because Jesus gave us the authority of the world and left the world so we can manifest from God through His name, Jesus.

You must take ownership of it and **KNOW** you are entitled to receive from the Father who loves you and wants you to have all things. When you buy a home you have a vision of what you want, you seek out the house, you find it, and you buy it, get the keys (take ownership) and move in. You have a deed to the house to show that it is yours. That is how manifestation works. There is a catch though; you have to pay for the house! It is yours to have but you must make the payment

> **2 Corinthians 9:6-7.** *But I SAY, He that sows sparingly, shall also reap sparingly; and he that sows bountifully shall reap also bountifully. Every man according as he purposes in his heart, so let him give: For God loves a cheerful giver.*

A New Age of God

This passage has been interpreted to be about money but read it again and think about love instead of money. To be loved you must love. When you love someone, you don't love them for what you can get; if you really love them you want to give them all you can to make them happy and they will receive your love and want to do for you.

The love of man for God is the key to God working through man.

Love is not about the self but about selflessness. Selflessness calls the love to you. It is better to give than receive and what you give comes back 100 fold. Forget about the money aspect and focus on love.

This is the key to worship and praise. You must give your love to God through worship and praise and you will receive it back 100 fold. The love you feel for God is the catalyst for your growth. You send Him all the love you have and He will return it magnified. The devotion you show God spurs God to your presence and to your mind. If you hunger for more love in your life this is the key to receiving.

As long as you are bound up in the self and focused on the self you will be living in within the self. Move out of the self and give Him the love that is His due and you will receive His love as your inheritance! Claim it and take ownership.

> **Hebrews 11:6.** *But without faith it is impossible to please Him: for he that comes to God must believe that He IS, and THAT He is a rewarder of them that diligently seek Him.*

A New Age of God

Faith is living through the Word. Diligently seek Him and send Him your love and the love you send comes back magnified and this is the process that God will use to change the demeanor of mankind.

Mankind must take the love of God that is waiting for them.

The evolution of the spirit is done through worshipping the Lord and sending your love to the spirit level. Once you start to send your love it is magnified by the Lord and returned to you. Stronger...*Larger*...**MAGNIFIED**. Here is where the love of the Father lives because the love of the Father is with you always and when the Holy Spirit dwells within you start receiving His love you will start to wonder if your heart can take it all in.

Just as God does not give you works you cannot do; He does not send more love than you can handle. When God works with you to expand what you can do you are growing in ability and confidence, well that is the way it works in love as well. As you receive your heart will grow and expand its capacity to love and receive love.

God created the heaven and the Earth through word. This is the most basic of science of God principals of creation. Every word you say creates your world; it dictates your attitude and sets up what you expect to receive. What do you want out of your life? What do you want to create for yourself? It is up to you to make the decision on what life you want.

Jesus manifested His works by only speaking the words of the Father as it was given to Him; we need to speak the word of God to manifest our life, for through God all things are possible. We must believe the word, plant the seed of the word with joy and expectation and the

A New Age of God

say the word aloud. The power lies within the tongue to blend the act and bring it to life. You must call it into being on Earth and bind it to you through faith for it to manifest. The peace of Christ comes from knowing Jesus is handling everything for you.

You have the power to create or you can throw your blessings out the window by ignoring their importance. The absolute worst thing you can do is to say I believe but...that is a rebuttal of your faith and eliminates your faith in your blessings.

If you are a negative person that worries all the time about the bad possibilities in every situation you are destroying your blessings. If you live in fear you are not living a God kind of faith.

You might say that I just don't understand what you are going through. If you are under-going trials ask for deliverance and then put your faith in action. Satan loves it when we question God because fear destroys all your creative power because fear destroys faith. Satan wants to diminish your power and keep you under condemnation and at the mercy of his plans.

When the enemy whispers to you in the night and tells you how inadequate you are or how you will never change your life that is the enemy lying in your ear and poisoning your mind. Rebuke those thoughts and turn them into positive thoughts. Laugh in the face of doubt, use the name of Jesus against him and he will disappear as if he were only a puff of smoke.

> **Mark 4:15.** *And these are they by the wayside, where the word is sown; but when they have heard; Satan comes immediately and takes away the word that was sown in their hearts.*

Satan takes the power of the word from the unbeliever by planting doubt and scorn in the mind; but the word of God will control Satan. The enemy uses the intellectual mind to supplant anything in the supernatural realm of God. He strives to use the entertainment industry to convince us that the supernatural is the domain of the Devil.

Learn to trust in the Lord and your faith will blossom. You need to declare to the Lord what you want, say it, put it in your heart and believe. You don't have to understand how the process works…it will grow. You plant the seed, a blade will surface, a bud will blossom and it will bear fruit. Faith grows when it is used and when you place it in your heart and it will manifest.

> **Mark 4:26-27** *And Jesus said, "So is the kingdom of God, as if a man should cast seed into the ground, and should sleep, and rise night and day, and the seed should spring and grow up, he knows not how."*

The kingdom lies within, when you speak in believing you plant the seed within and as you sleep it takes root in the mind and the spirit. Then suddenly sometime in the future the seed grows into manifestation. Faith always works; use it in every aspect of your life. Faith grows, it starts as a seed which you plant in your heart and your heart will grow your words… Whatever you sow will grow because your spirit is made to grow the things you will into being.

How the word works:

The word was spoken (the seed was sown).

A New Age of God

While you sleep it grows and takes root in the spirit

Your excitement and enthusiasm fertilized the word

When it has matured it bears fruit at the proper time and season.

> **Genesis 1:3.** *And God said, "Let there be light" and there was light.*

Sounds and words created the world and you have created your world. Whether you intentionally create your world or not, you have the power and you are using it every day. Think about that for a moment. What has come out your mouth in the last 24 hours? What have you manifested? Did you speak a positive manifestation or a negative manifestation? Remember what comes from the mouth is a double edged sword! It is a sword that can create or it can destroy depending on how it is used.

God created the heavens and the Earth through the spoken word. He said let there be light and there was light. Well not only did He create us in his image but he has endowed us with the same power to create our lives. Jesus said that we could do all that He did and more. This is the quantum physics of GOD. We have been seduced by the ego and the logical mind to believe the fallacy that all there is, is what we can see and feel. All that exists in the universe is what lies before us. What we think generates what we say and what we say creates our world.

Your mind believes what your mouth says. Every word you speak in praise is also accepted by the conscious and subconscious mind and reinforces your belief. It is up to you; your words can either build you up or tear down your relationships. Once it is out of your mouth you

A New Age of God

cannot take it back. There should be a slight pause before you speak to give yourself the chance to reevaluate and censor your words before you speak.

Think of your spiritual journey as a quest; just like preparing to climb a mountain. You build up your muscles to ready yourself for the climb. With each climb you get stronger and eventually you get strong enough to reach to a new level and you get closer to the summit.

If you are hungry for more of God, if you have had visions from the Spirit realm, you are not alone. If you wish to have visions you can open yourself up through prayer and the word of God. God is calling His chosen ones; HE is waiting to awaken the God spark that each of us holds within because it is waiting for you to spark into a real life. God has been working in my life for 30 years urging me to do more, to dig deeper and further into the kingdom and bring Gods case to His people who lay sleeping waiting to be aroused awake.

People have been run out of churches by the attitudes of the pastors and the congregations. They are bogged down by law and empty prayers; sitting in judgment and criticism. Here comes a seeker looking to be moved by God, going looking for the eyes, arms and heart of Christ to welcome them into the family and wind up feeling rejected and disappointed. You should never leave church as you came; each experience should grow your faith and spirit. It is time to accept the will of God, live the message Jesus came and died to give and build up a church that walks the walk and talks the talk offering a spiritual relationship with the Lord God to the whole world. The wrong attitude or the wrong words can drive away the people you need to join you to do Gods work.

That is why you need to be careful of what you say, try to take a couple of seconds to review your words because your mind believes every word you say. People's

A New Age of God

impression of you comes from how you present yourself and how you speak to them. They judge your attitude from the words you say and how you say them. Take a minute and observe your demeanor, your attitude and what you say on a regular basis. Most people do not look at how they present themselves and don't give a second thought about what they say. If you are so self-absorbed and sullen with you own troubles, how can you reach out to help someone else? Love shows on your face just as a spirit of disapproval and judgment shows.

Most depressed people feed themselves negative information on a constant basis; they are stuck in a loop rethinking the same feelings and thoughts and with each pass of the recording the emotions get more and more intense; you feel more and more alone as the thoughts get darker and more hopeless.

If a person says one thing and does another they are at cross purposes, and they erase all the work they have attempted to achieve. It's like the dieter that follows the program all week long but goes crazy eating all weekend long. Then he wonders why he never loses any weight. You must steer yourself in a steady course or you will wind up taking one step forward and two steps back, constantly being in confusion and living in frustration.

When you pray in faith and belief then walk in doubt, worry and fear, your prayers may not be answered because you have shown a lack of faith. Fear dissolves faith and your prayers dissipate in the wind. If you say you pray every day and none of your prayers are ever answered then you need to look at your life and see where you are lacking. Examine your life and decide if the way you are living is as it should be or perhaps the cause could be doubt and fear or maybe you just don't believe they will be answered. Maybe those prayers were

A New Age of God

answered but you do not realize it because you received what you needed not what you prayed for.

Control of your mind, emotions and your actions is essential to your progress. Your emotions want to control you and your actions but you have a choice in how you think and how you respond to situations. You must choose what you will allow yourself to react to and guard what you feed your mind just as you choose what you put in your body. Everything you watch what music you listen to, or what you read effects your state of mind. You are undertaking to alter the way you think and to take responsibility for your thoughts and actions and it will be an awesome experience. In 12 months you will be amazed in the changes you will have accomplished.

What we fail to realize is as we focus on the material world, we become more and more grounded in carnality (emotional living) and we get farther and farther from our Source which is God. We pollute our minds with the garbage of Madison Ave and the filth of television and movies.

The junk the world provides for our minds is just like the food that pollutes our bodies with chemicals and preservatives, not to mention that we consume tons of sugar in everything. It is expensive and difficult to feed your body with whole nutritious food and keep up with the rat race of our lives. That is why we need to simplify our lives.

We keep running as fast as we can, trying to keep up with unattainable goals that keep moving farther away from our grasp. It is like the carrot on the string in front of the donkey to keep it moving down the road. We make excuses why we cannot make time to dedicate any of our time to training our minds; there is no time to study God's word or to meditate on God's plan. Yet there is a plan laid out a for us; there is a plan for the universe but

A New Age of God

we are so addicted to the 50 inch television, the video games or the shiny new car and all the bogus toys that we are convinced we need to keep us entertained and keep us happy. We are not what we own!

When was the last time you just sat quietly and just thought about things? Can you just be still and wait? Can you stand to be alone with yourself? Do you like yourself?

Our minds convince us the path to happiness is paved with things. Our thoughts create our attitude and our emotions urge us to amass more and more useless stuff in the search for contentment. We must strive to master our minds and emotions if we want to create a better world. Emotions and moods are fed by the lies of the ego and rationalize what we do.

The ego and our emotions are used by the enemy to keep us in the dark. That is why so many people are stuck crying out in the dark for some meaning in their life. You cannot buy happiness with a credit card and it definitely isn't in a bottle of booze. The ego is the doorway that allows the enemy into our hearts and mind. If you live in the land of the ego then you live all alone thinking only of yourself and your happiness. Everything you see is from the perspective of the self and you become mired in selfishness. Feelings of superiority and prejudice are weapons Satan uses to keep us separated from each other and from God.

Our God spark was planted within our Spirit upon our creation and it can only be awakened through a change in attitude, in our diet and in our spiritual life through prayer, praise and meditation. There lays within each of us a deep spiritual well, just waiting to come to life and overflow in abundance. Your cup can and shall run over and goodness and love will fill all your days. Each of us can achieve a level of happiness that most people only dream of. Jesus is the spring that runs eternal.

A New Age of God

> **John 14:23** *And Jesus said unto him: If a man love me and keep my words: and my Father will love him, and we will come unto him, and make our abode with him.*

If you are working on change then you will be remade so you must be prepared for a little rebellion from within. We live as prisoners of our subconscious mind and the mind does not like change. You must recognize the method of the attack that comes from within to stop you from changing. Learn to rebuke the inner voice that seeks to drag you down and keep you mired in the past.

There is a series of steps you can take to work your way within to find your inner sanctum of happiness. First of all you must want to seek the face of God within yourself working through with the Holy Spirits help. There must be a hunger for truth, a deep longing that needs to be fulfilled.

Second, you must clean up your mind and take responsibility for your thoughts. If you keep your mind and your eyes on God it will be easier to move your thoughts in the right direction. Third, be mindful of what music you listen to the movies and programs you watch. The mind is like a computer, if you feed computer programs garbage the data that comes out is garbage. You are the keeper of the gate to your mind and you must be on guard.

Try listening to classical new age or Christian music and eliminate anything that pollutes your mind. There is alternate entertainment than some of the garbage there is out there.

Fourth, clean up your body: alcohol, drugs and caffeine pollute the body and the mind. Consider the antibiotics and hormones that are given to most of the feed animals

A New Age of God

these days. Your temple is your body and you must learn to treat it with respect. The quality of your physical body is what you have to live in while you are here. How healthy you eat helps determine how clearly you think. Sugar affects your blood sugar levels, which affects your hormone levels. You need a stable mind body and spirit. Whole foods feed the whole body. I repeat your body is your temple and you must respect your temple.

Your mind wants things to remain the same and stay in the same old routine. Habits are a strong force in our lives and change takes you out of your comfort zone. This process will make you uncomfortable something like walking around in new shoes that are a little tight. Sometimes it even manifests in physical reactions which might feel like anxiety attacks, but just knowing that this is natural will help you know that it is to be expected. It is caused by changes within in the Spirit and is usually felt when the Holy Spirit is working on your evolution to a new level of alignment. This process happens every time you step to a new level of spiritual consciousness. It helps to be prepared and understand what to expect.

Your mind believes what you say. Just thinking your payers is not enough; yes the Lord hears your every thought, hears your prayers and knows your needs. You are working on reprogramming your attitude to reach new levels. You must train yourself to tell your mind out loud what you want it to believe. It is essential for you to make this a habit every day, especially the first thoughts of the day. Your first thoughts and actions dictate how your day will go. Take a couple of minutes before you get up to focus your mind on God and to be grateful for the new day and the challenges and opportunities you know God will put before you.

If you develop this habit you will see a definite change in how your day goes. Know what you want out of your

A New Age of God

day, thank God for giving it to you and believe you have already received it. The result will be amazing before you know it.

You must assume the responsibility to guard your words and make sure you do not contradict yourself because if you send mixed messages you will be putting your mind into a state of confusion. Please, please, please take this into your heart and believe it. So many people waste their time and energy destroying the possibilities in their lives. They analyze everything, doubt all they hear, doubt all they do and have no confidence in their own abilities and do not allow God to provide what the truly need.

If you are one of these people please stop it now, do not allow yourself to be kept in turmoil. Don't be a rudderless boat at the mercy of the storm, being blown hither and yon until you find yourself crashing on the rocks. Without a rudder a boat cannot be guided and even though they may see the light of the lighthouse warning them of the rocks, there is nothing they can do to stop the boat.

If you live with someone who questions everything and is constantly doubting all you do and diminishing your faith you will have to realize you are only responsible for your own faith and all you can do is lead by example. Do not feel like you will have to have a double portion faith to help drag them along the way. Each of us is responsible for the care and maintenance of our spirit and our body.

You will have to ask the Holy Spirit for the strength to have a single-minded faith and be willing to be steadfast every day. You must keep your heart and mind on God. All you can do is become a guiding light to help them find the way. Marriages fail because of this countering effect of separate beliefs; you need to be a team pulling together for the same purpose, to work for the same cause is

A New Age of God

essential. Allow the Holy Spirit to work through you to lead your family to the Lord.

We understand that we are designed to be self-programmable so we may grow what we sow. What do you want to grow? Do you want to do the works of God? Therein lies the key to your destiny; there's nothing you cannot do! If you have a calling it is time to answer your call.

If you have a dream you can bring it to life. If there was ever a time that needs everyone to step up and help it is now. The world needs everyone to take a step in faith and start to answer the call. If you only change the world in a three foot radius around then you have changed your world and possibly have started a chain reaction with all the people you touch. It is time to start doing the works of God.

CHAPTER 4

Works of God

Genesis 1:26 *And God said, let us make man in our image, after our likeness: and let them have dominion over the fish of the sea, and over the foul of the air, and over the cattle, and over all the earth, and over every creeping thing that creeps upon the earth.*

God has a covenant with man and when He gave man dominion over the Earth He relegated the works on Earth to mankind. God will utilize man to achieve His works on Earth until Jesus returns to reign at the end of days. God has a Devine plan for mankind and that is why He gave us the power to have dominion. God made that covenant and He cannot go back on His commitments.

That is why Jesus had to be born in the flesh of man in order to do Gods work on Earth. Jesus had to be born of the flesh and walk with us to perform His miracles and touch our lives. God is calling people into service in order to manifest change, whether it is to perform a miracle or to help the world have change in attitude, he must have

A New Age of God

a human being to work through. Many are called into service but few are willing to step out in faith and do the will of God to manifest His works.

People use the horrible things that go on in the world to prove there is no God, but these terrible things happen because man through free will has allowed them to occur. We have been given free will and the power of manifestation so that we have the ability to create wonders and change the world.

The other side of the coin of free will is that man can perform abominations or allow things to happen through a mistaken attitude that says it's not his business. We cannot blame God for the state of the world. We live in a world where 1 in 5 people have been abused when they were children. Human trafficking and slavery still goes on to this day. We must step up and take responsibility for our own mess and stand up and stop these horrible things and restore this world to its intended state.

It is time for us to answer the call and start to do the works of God. There's a process that will awaken you to your purpose that will direct you to do the works of God. First and foremost you must have the desire to serve God.

> **John 14:12-13.** *Verily, verily, I say unto you, He that believes on me, the works that I do shall he do also; and greater works shall he do; because I go on to the Father. And whatsoever you shall ask, ask in my name, that I will do that the Father may be glorified in the Son.*

The works of God is that you believe in Him in all you do. There is no problem that cannot be solved... Be in Christ! You as a believer must let the word teach and instruct you because it will go against the physical mind but the

A New Age of God

spirit will receive and begin to process the Word within the heart.

Your soul self will fight this process, your logical mind will fight this and that is where the faith factor comes into play to create what you want. You are transforming in the spirit realm and the logical mind cannot grasp the creativeness and concepts of God.

The closest explanation man has come up with is quantum physics to explain how a desire combined with faith and belief can be manifested. Science is striving to explain the unexplainable when there is no need to have an equation to make it real. The fact that it works is affirmed by their attempt to explain how it is done. Mankind has far more power and ability than we give ourselves credit for. Through the power of the higher-self working with the Holy Spirit man can change the world.

My Pastor, Todd Brown was mentored and trained by his Father-in-law here in Texas. This man was known for his absolute faith in Jesus. One of my favorite events was when there was a woman in his congregation had a large cancer on her face that looked terrible and it oozed and seeped all the time. She stopped going to church because she knew it bothered the other members of the congregation just to look at her and it made her feel uncomfortable.

He asked her to come back to church, he told her it did not matter to God what she looked like, all He cared about was her faith and God wanted her presence in church; the congregation could deal with it. That next Sunday she came to church and sat in her regular place and during his sermon the Lord moved the Pastor into action; leaping over the rail he pulled out his handkerchief and spoke, "In the name of Jesus I rebuke this cancer and command it to be gone from this woman's

A New Age of God

face; I cast you out!", he placed the handkerchief on the cancer as he rebuked Satan and demanded the cancer be gone from her face. *THE CANCER FELL INTO THE HANDKERCHIEF FROM HER FACE. THERE WAS NO SCAR OR ANY EVIDENCE IT WAS EVER THERE.* Faith healed her, his faith in what God moved him to do and her faith in what was possible through the Lord. This was not an uncommon occurrence in that church, the Lord used that man to perform mighty acts of faith and people came from all over Texas for his ministering. There are too many incidences where miracles happened to relate here but be assured; faith performs miracles right now for those people who seek Him in faith and believing! God does miraculous things where people of likeminded faith agree together. If you have the faith of a child anything can happen. Whenever two or more gather together in agreement in faith it will be done.

> **John 8:54.** *If I honor myself, my honor is nothing: it is my Father that honors me; of whom you say that He is your God*
>
> **John 9:4-5.** *I must work the works of Him that sent me, while it is day: the night comes, when no man can work. As long as I am in the world I am the light of the world.*

Once you are born again in faith, you become a new person and your possibilities are limitless. Christianity is the only faith where God lives within. God loves to step out and show His presence for those who believe. God operates in the supernatural and Satan is trying to convince you that the time of miracles has passed and the Lord no longer works as He did in biblical times. Satan

A New Age of God

wants to stop the supernatural from occurring on Earth, because he knows that:

1. One demonstration of a miracle is worth 100,000 sermons
2. People crave miracles in their lives
3. Satan knows that miracles separate the people from dead gods

1John 4:4. *You are of God, little children and have overcome them, because greater is He that is in you, than he is in the world.*

Jesus died on the cross, and God opened up the heavens. The veil was torn that separated God and man. This allowed the Holy Spirit to become present on the Earth. After 3 days Christ rose from the crypt and taught and preached to his disciples and believers for 40 days, before He ascended into heaven; he then assumed the Mercy Seat and became the intercessor for man with God. Jesus sits at God's right hand awaiting each and every one of us. Jesus was the Son of God and He lived a life that he transcended death. Man in his original state also had the pure essence of the creator and death was not a factor in his life. Once he was contaminated with the carnal nature man lost the ability to transcend to the spiritual realm.

We could regain that purity if we could move past the animal within. It has happened before and a rare few have transcended to be with the Lord. Only those who walk in absolute unity with the Father can achieve this miraculous state.

Each and every human being at the end of this life will have to face the life they have led. When you walk to the Throne of God the path you take will be paved with all the love you have given during your stay on this Earth. When you approach the Book of Life and stand face to face with our Lord how glorious will your walk be? What will you have created? What will the Lord see recorded in that Holy Book when you stand before the works of your life?

Understand that you are building your next life right here and now. Regardless of your choice you have one life eternal. There is no death; you transcend this life into your true self in God. What life do you want to live through eternity? Do you want to achieve a higher level in heaven?

What you do now must be done as if the Savior were physically there with you, for you know that He is with you always...Keep in mind you never walk alone. You have Guardians, guides and teachers; Angels of God that have dedicated their existence to being there for you.

You are the creation of the Almighty; a product of God's love. You are made to be a product of love, a part of the Law of the Eternal one, made to be God on Earth. The Son of God came and walked this Earth; all He did was done to show you how to live. All His suffering was endured so that you could be shown the possibility of what YOU can do.

You *MUST* face the fact that you are eternal, whether you live within God's love or you turn your back on God. Imagine standing before the throne, in the presence of the Almighty, experiencing absolute love and being cast away, shunned from the Light, and being cast into isolation. Imagine the hurt He will experience from the disappointment he will feel.

Imagine Him looking at you and seeing a tear roll down in his cheek because as he must put you aside. You MUST face the fact that you are eternal, whether you live with God or you shun his love. What if every day, throughout

A New Age of God

eternity, you live seeing others living on in bliss while you exist in the torment of separation?

Imagine paradise; everyone you know in sight; but you can't touch them or hear them but you can see everything you can't have. Your life will be darkness and separation, devoid of God's grace. That is my vision of Hell, because there could be no greater torment for me than to live in separation from my sweet Jesus who is my Lord and Savior. He is the air I breathe and the light that guides my life.

There is a consequence to how you live. The atheist that believes this is all there is will wind up at the same place as you and me. You may create the circumstances that you live in for eternity but God will decide what Hell you deserve for your life.

The Lord gave me a vision to help me understand what we will all see when we pass from this life. I have recorded the events as close to what I saw as possible.

A Walk to the Throne

Each life is recorded in the Holy Akashic Records in God's kingdom. When you receive the Holy Spirit you are recorded in the book of life.

You are in a beautiful garden. Everything is the most vibrant colors you have ever seen. The sky is the color of azure blue. Trees standing 50' tall were lining a path that leads to a crystal blue lake. There is a babbling brook that flows into the lake that looks like it is made of crushed pearls and jewels that stretches into the distance. Far off high above on a hill top you see a golden glowing throne and you feel compelled to follow the path. Beautiful

A New Age of God

music and chimes are playing within the light breeze that caresses your skin.

A man, walks by wearing a beautiful robe that shimmers and sparkles in the sunlight his smile is radiant, he is almost dancing along he is so full of joy. He has lived for this day for many, many years. He worked hard to raise a family and lead all he knew in righteousness and love. He was a success in his work and in his life. He lived his life among the blessings of God. He is glowing with happiness and expectation. He is greeted by a man dressed in a pure white robe trimmed in purple, which embraces him and offers to join him on his walk up the path of life.

Lagging far behind is a second man, wearing a gray gown, shuffling slowly along and as he walks the path changes and becomes dull and dusty. With each step he throws up a little cloud of dry dust; he is frowning and there is a look of dread and remorse with tears trickling down his face. Each step seems to be forced as if it takes effort to continue. There is no one to greet him; this walk he must make alone because that is how he led his life, a solitary man whose only concern was for his own little world and what he owned. He was always so proud of his accomplishments. On Earth he had owned a mansion, had a beautiful young woman on his arm, always driving fine cars and was a ruthless businessman. He took great pride in those business deals that took advantage of others, seeking profit at any cost. He taught his children to live for their possessions and to always know who they were and where they came from. He taught his children to keep to their own class and to get what they wanted no matter what it took.

Now that he was here it was a different story, he has to stand on his merit and how he lived. He had to stand without possessions or money but on the merit of his heart.

A New Age of God

As they proceed along they cross a golden bridge that arched crosses the stream and the path continues to the throne. The throne can be seen from every point of the horizon, sitting high upon a hill. It looks as if it is made of precious gems and gold glittering in the distance. There is an aura to the throne that is indescribable and it acts like a magnet drawing all who arrive to hurry to the presence. Sitting to the right hand of the throne sits Jesus on His mercy seat. Angels surround the throne singing praise for the King in all His glory.

The first man is greeted at the throne amid joyous laughter and celebration. The air rings with beautiful music and Angelic voices are lifted in praise and welcome. He has come home and his family rejoices at his arrival. He is embraced and escorted to the book of records where his life is recorded in bold gold script. Jesus looks at him with joy and absolute love and welcomes him, reading aloud all his good works and recounting his love for the Father. Jesus embraces the man and escorts him to the gates that lead into the kingdom.

The second man shuffles up to the throne, where he must relive the life he has led and he is filled with shame. Jesus is filled with remorse and a tear falls down his cheek. Jesus shows him where his name is not written in the book of life and gently embraces the man and escorts him from the book; the realization hits that he is being denied entry to the kingdom. This grieves Jesus to have to cast another out of paradise and send him away. This person has thrown away his chance to live with the King and be surrounded with abundance and joy. He will have to endure separation from the love and compassion, not to be allowed entry.

Do not live your life as a leper that cannot touch or live with those who are alive. Jesus healed the lepers, through faith in Him; to show those who live without faith are lepers in the Spirit. Healed they were rejoined with love and life so they could eat at the table of life and be shunned no more.

One love, one life eternal, you create your life here and in eternity with your words, your attitude, your thoughts and your actions. The Holy Spirit is waiting for all who will be cleansed and offers their love to God and want to see Gods promise in all things.

A matter of belief

Who we are is the sum of who we believe we are. The main question is; are we who we have been told we are by our parents, teachers, and ministers and not least of all the media? Who are you really? Are you the person you want to be?

I was a child of the fifties, where a female had to fit certain profile and had to look and act a certain way. There was no physical abuse but my parents made sure you knew you were not good enough. If you made straight A's then you had no common sense. If you wanted to better yourself then you were ashamed of where you came from. My sister was the pretty one, always the perfect little girl with her long blonde hair and a perfect figure. I was fat a kid and smart but I was isolated from any positive encouragement. I never believed in myself and had severe self-esteem issues. For the first 22 years of my life I never felt loved or wanted by my family. This caused me to make more mistakes than I care to go into.

The subconscious mind is a sponge recording all we see, hear and experience and we have all that cycling through our minds over and over and over. We have about 50 basic thoughts that we repeat constantly in one form or

A New Age of God

another. Most are really just an echo of the past replaying in our mind.

Our programming began all the way back in the womb. From the fetus on we are constantly learning and developing into who we are. In the womb we live a symbiotic life with the Mother. All the stress of everyday of the Mothers life is passed on; it is all passed on; the anxieties as well as the happiness and the laughter. If Mama isn't feeling loved and happy then the baby shares all those feelings.

There is scientific proof of how anxiety is passed on to the baby. A research group did an ultrasound on a fetus while the parents were having an argument and the reactions of the baby were witnessed. The baby literally went into distress and at the end of the argument they smashed a vase and the baby literally lurched and completely arched its back as if thrown backwards.

So we are not only a victim of genetics and evolution, but a product of our family environment beginning back to our very conception. To the point that it matters how we were conceived in a moment of passion, a situation of complacency or God forbid even an act of violence. Whether we passed nine months in health and happy expectation or the time was passed with worry and anxiety the baby holds on to those feelings. After they are born babies need to bond with the Mother and feel safe and loved; if we do not receive this love and bonding the result is severe psychological damage that ends with a person that is unable to love and this has resulted in serial killers such as Ted Bundy.

It is up to us as a society how we choose to raise our children. Do you want your children raised by videos and video games as baby sitters? The influences of the world are unspeakable and if you don't take responsibility for what your family is exposed to, and what they believe in;

A New Age of God

I despair for their future. How can we change the world if we can't change how we live in our own little world?

Do you want to do the works of God? Do you want to change the world? Do you want to make a difference, or are you willing to leave it to the other guy? Well guess what, they aren't doing such a good job of it so far. It is time to step up and be counted.

My prayer is for you to be a person that walks in Christ every day of your life, that you keep your eyes on God, and in the future people who have known you for years start saying; who is this person I see before me? I have known them for years yet I do not recognize the person before me! That is because a new person in Christ has been made. For if they believe on Him and in Him and He has remade them in HIS Spirit to walk the Earth. You too can be washed clean and your past can be erased. You can start a new life in Christ, regardless of your past.

We seem to be living in a time of extremists, even within the Christian religion; there seem to be a stringent intolerance of anyone who does not fit their profile exactly. Jesus came to unify, to unite the Jews with the Gentiles and to live in peace. We must first and foremost be the representatives of Christ on earth, if we are to do His work and in His name we must follow His teachings and unify in the name of Christ.

We must assume the Messianic Spirit of Jesus. This is a highly evolved spiritual level that dictates we work for a unity as a people and have an unending compassion for the world at large. In the first century there was a Messianic movement which merged the Jews and the Gentiles in which some Jewish priests adopted the doctrines of Christ. All evidence of their activities seems to have been subverted and locked away. They were known as the first Nazarene (Messianic) church and their

A New Age of God

seal consisted of a Menorah on top, a Star of David in the center and a fish at the bottom.

It signified the unity of the Jew and Gentile who were brought together by Christ on the cross. Jesus wanted the feud between the Jews and Gentiles to come to an end and for them to live in peace under the Blood of the Cross which was shed to bring peace. HE died to bring peace and unity and man has used that ultimate act of sacrifice to persecute the Jews for thousands of years. The Jews have steadfastly refused to consider Jesus as the Messiah; perhaps He did not fit their image of who the Messiah would be. They wanted a deliver from Rome and Jesus came to deliver man from himself.

A lack of love and faith has allowed the enemy to use Jesus' life to be used for evil purposes. How many wars have been fought in the Prince of Peace's name? Hitler would have never been allowed to commit the Holocaust if there had not been anger and distrust of the Jews for 2000 years over the crucifixion. Separation from Gods mandate for tolerance and peace and self-righteousness have allowed millions of people to have been killed in the name of Jesus.

We as Christians must be tolerant of other faiths and allow them to witness our faith in action. Guide them by our love and proof that we love a living, compassionate God and not by our hate and distrust of them. We cannot assume we are superior in rights to anyone but on the other hand we cannot give up our right to be Christians. Christians come in all flavors and colors, none of us are perfect and we must allow God to be the judge of another's actions. We need to reach out to all denominations of our own Christian faith and drop the attitude that one is any more correct than the other. If they accept Jesus as their Lord and Savior then they are fellow Christians.

A New Age of God

We must reach out to the Jewish people and celebrate our similarities instead of our differences. All Jesus did was predestined to bring us together. Don't you think it is time we started to try to accomplish what he started? Let's start to practice what we should be preaching!

All people are welcome in God's house. There are many gays and lesbians who love the Lord and want to live a Christian life. They have as much right to sit in worship as we do. I know the Bible speaks against it but we cannot exclude them from their right to find their way in God. That is between them and God and we must be tolerant. If we sit in judgment, then we will be judged even more severely by our own standards.

How many people sit in church every Sunday that go against something in the Bible? Don't they have the right to worship and get the teachings and guidance of God? Let's open our hearts and include all of mankind in our doors. Jesus mandated that we love everyone as we love ourselves. He did not say love only those ones that agree with you or those that look and act like you. Let God be the judge and let Him convict those He sees living in error. We need to live a righteous life but beware of living a self-righteous life; self-righteousness is leaving the door wide open for Satan to manipulate your ego, make you feel superior, and judgmental and separate you from God.

It's not easy or comfortable to open your heart to people who go against your own personal beliefs or morals, but Jesus never said it would be easy, He just said it was right. He believed in talking and eating with sinners so He could bring them back to God's flock. It is like being an American and allowing free speech from people who make your blood boil; if we take away their rights then we must forfeit our rights too. If we deny freedom to worship from anyone then we are opening the door to lose our rights too. We must stand for Christ in all our actions and deeds.

Separation of church and state in America is one big lie. America was founded on freedom of religion not freedom from religion. Most of our founding fathers were Deists, which means they did not believe in the Divinity of Jesus. They might have not been in agreement on the specifics of God but they were adamant about being free to worship. We are one Nation under God and our government must operate in a Godly manner. We cannot stand by and allow our country to leave its founding Fathers ideals. We must stand up for Christ in our homes, our schools and in our country! To do the works of God we must stand up for God in our own communities and we must vote our beliefs.

CHAPTER 5

Spirit Filled

John 3:5-8 *Verily, verily, I say unto thee, except a man is born of water and of the HOLY SPIRIT, he cannot enter into the kingdom of GOD. That which is born of the flesh is flesh; and all that is born of the Spirit is Spirit. Marvel not that I said unto you, you must be born again.*

John 4:23-24 *Jesus said, "But the hour comes, and now is, when the true worshippers shall worship The Father in spirit and in truth: for the Father seeks such to worship Him. God is a spirit: and they that worship HIM must worship HIM in spirit and in truth".*

The keys to learning to live the Jesus Way is through developing a daily routine that starts your day with God and keeps Him with you throughout your day. You need to organize your day so you may start reading the word every day out loud, pray daily preferably out loud, praise out loud and meditate. Meditation on God will cause you

A New Age of God

to start having spiritual experiences as it opens the door to your inner being.

It is imperative that you worship the Lord out loud whenever you can. It may seem awkward at first if you were raised to do your worshipping quietly but it will help you to intensify your faith. I keep an ongoing conversation with the Lord all day long affirming my love and my covenant with Him. I speak to the Lord as if I am talking to my best friend.

When you dedicate yourself to a new spiritual life you will begin to become alive in spirit and you will build your faith and begin living a whole new existence. The Apostle Paul speaks at great length in the Acts of the Apostles about casting off the old dead self and becoming a new man in Christ. There are things that you will need to do to keep growing in spirit. When Paul speaks of the living in death, he is speaking of walking without God is a life in darkness of spirit and therefore dead. When you are alive you are living in spirit and light. That is the emptiness people speak about when they are trying to figure out the purpose for life. The book of St. John speaks of the great Comforter.

The Comforter is the Holy Spirit that brings comfort and guidance when you decide to receive the gift of the Holy Spirit and walk it the light and love of God.

To live the Jesus Way requires you to be honest with yourself about who you were before you came to Christ and who you want to be in Christ. You need to see yourself and others with new eyes and come to terms with changes you will need to make both within the self and the changes needed in your world. When you are honest with yourself you will be able to pin point the areas that need to change and the areas that need prayer for the Holy Spirit to help you change. As a person thinks is how

A New Age of God

they will end up. You need a clear vision of the person you want to be and where you want to go.

How can you start a new life in Christ and wear the rags of the old man?

Cast off the old rags and accept the new raiment. Allow the joy of the Lord to show. Rejoice in your life and show the world what God has done to remake you. The new man conquers the old. The word, praise and prayer are the steps to joy. Open your heart and stop trying to figure things out for yourself. God knows your needs and has them waiting for you in Heaven. All you have to do is submit to His authority, claim the inheritance of your Father and call down your blessings. This is submitting to God's will and authority. There is a light at the end of the tunnel and that light is God; for He is the Light and the Way. Put nothing before God; put no one before God. Treasure the love in your life.

Depression is the fog Satan uses to block the Light and the Way. He wants to keep you in darkness. His favorite tool is money to keep you bound in the chains of despair. The key to lifting the fog is to praise the Lord for your life and for all He has given you. If God is putting you through trials it is to get you to seek the light and give it over to Him. The enemy has no power over the dominion of the Lord and all you have to do is submit and be grateful and the fog will begin to lift and the Light will burn through just like the rising sun burns away the fog in the light of morning. The darkness of the night always passes and the light of the morning prevails on the darkness.

> **John 5:14-15:** *And this is the confidence that we have in Him, that, if we ask anything according to*

A New Age of God

> *His will, He will hear us: and if we know that He hears us, whatsoever we ask, we have the petitions that we desired of Him.*

I worked for 20 years driving a big rig over the road with my husband. Every day I was exposed to the worst parts of humanity and some of the best. I was alone in my faith except for my husband. I spent most of my drive time focusing on the Lord and seeking what I needed to do to find my way to give back for all He had done for me. I kept Him on my heart and my mind by listening to Christian music or books on CD. The longer I stayed within this routine the more I was compelled to honor my faith and step up for God.

Once I received the Holy Spirit it became harder and harder for me to continue in that world. I needed to be full time in devotion and spending my time with people of like mind to keep my precious new life intact and growing. I needed the reinforcement that comes from regular worship and study. In the truck it was almost impossible to find a quiet time to be alone for prayer and meditation and developing an atmosphere of worship was elusive at best. The pull to be at home to do His work became impossible to ignore. My Father was calling me to His work and I finally came home in faith even though I had no idea what it was He wanted me to do.

You too will need to find a way of life that allows you to focus on your growth and find people who will help you to walk in the light and continue to grow in faith. If you pray for God to send you the right people for your life, you will start to make the right friends and build relationships.

Revelation 3:15-16. *I know your works, that you are neither cold nor hot; I would that you were*

A New Age of God

> *cold or hot. So then because you are lukewarm, and neither cold nor hot, will I spew you out of my mouth.*

A word of caution you cannot hold on to the old and build the new, eventually you will make the leap to a life that encourages your life instead of holding you back. God does not want you to straddle the fence; you must be either hot or cold. God wants you to make a decision.

Miracles become possible and begin to manifest, you will never walk alone again and you will find a peace in His love that is unexplainable. I wish with all my heart I could tell you how I feel when I am in prayer or when I am praising Him. There is an emotional surge that brings me to tears and I feel His Omnipresence surrounding me. I know that all things are possible and I am so unworthy of such tremendous love.

I live in anticipation for His touch, for a small time of perfect love. In those moments I feel like my heart will burst from joy and love. I want everyone to have a taste of that perfect love of God.

There is a perfect balance that mankind is designed to function in and that is what I call our essence. Jesus operated every day in His essence and had a perfect relationship with the Father. God created man in that perfect balance of essence and when man walked in the Garden he had no expiration date. God expected for us to be with Him physically for an unlimited time.

When man became aware of guilt and shame it began to throw off the balance in the spirit and the body in which God has created it for. That is why early man lived so long in the Old Testament but as we began to move farther and farther from God and the animal contamination grew stronger and stronger the body went out of alignment. The body began to age at a more rapid pace.

A New Age of God

The animal awareness gave birth to a passion that has no equal, which was contrary to nature and changed the balance of the actual matter of the body. This caused a disturbance in the whole body which began to throw it out of alignment from its true balance. That is why Jesus can say peace is with you and peace will reside within. Peace is a life without fear, knowing that you walk with the Lord.

Jesus came to get man back to his basic essence. The more you walk in worry, doubt or even lust you take your body further and further out of sync with the universal balance, The doctors have proven that anger and worry cause cancer. Stress causes high blood pressure and ulcers. This is living proof that if you live out of the alignment of peace within then you will age more quickly and develop more diseases.

Faith is a knowing you will be taken care of; meditation helps lower your stress and allows you to bring yourself closer and closer to alignment as well as opens you up to spiritual experiences. Love and praise help balance your endorphin levels and brings you closer in alignment. Alignment brings you closer and closer to the place Jesus wanted you to operate in on a daily basis. You will be restoring your natural essence and allowing yourself to assume the power in partnership with God as was predestined.

That is why you are to be of good single minded, and not allow anyone to lead you astray. The son of man lives within you and you must keep your eyes on Him and be guided by the Holy Spirit.

Jesus wants each and every one of us to share the kingdom but it is your choice whether you live the life you were meant to live or if you fritter away your life on imaginary things. We choose whether to be of this world (the illusion of what you see is all there is) or choose a

A New Age of God

spirit filled life and live in this world but be not of this world (allowing the Holy Spirit to open your eyes to the true world).

The thing about Jesus is he walked in the spirit, aligned with the Father every day. He was in constant contact with the Father every moment. He did not have to ask for what He needed because He understood that the Father provides what you need. Jesus told God what He wanted and He knew the Father would provide. What we consider miracles Jesus thought of His manifestations as a part of His life and His ministry.

One day Jesus was hungry and He passed a barren fig tree, angry it was producing no fruit, He cursed the tree. Upon passing the tree on His trip back the next day, the Apostles were astounded when they saw that the fig tree had withered and died from the roots up in one day from being cursed.

A person was dead for four days and the body was starting to decompose, He called and the person was restored in perfect health. He created what He wanted through His Father and eliminated the useless. Jesus has little patience for that which bears no fruit. How marvelous it would be to have the same abilities as Christ! According to Christ's teachings, everything He did on Earth, we can do also even if we only have faith the size of a mustard seed.

Walk in in the Spirit, be one with Christ reach the goal that awaits each and every person. We should live in an age of miracles each and every day. If we model our lives on His word, His actions and His love we too can live the life of miracles.

God gave man authority on the Earth and that is why Jesus came to earth as a man. God needed someone to come to Earth so His children could witness the miracles

A New Age of God

of God on Earth and believe. Jesus knew the power of witnessing God manifesting miracles in the flesh.

Once we believe and take possession of the knowledge and ability, the following will be as obvious as 1, 2, and 3:

- God gave authority over all this world to man
- God used the word to form the universe
- God demands you to be single-minded in faith and action

We will be equipped to do His work and manifest miracles so the people will be able once again to witness God in action on the Earth.

To be one with Christ we must strive to have constant focus with Him. Pray unceasingly during your day, talk out loud to the Lord as if you are having a conversation with a friend. Attempt to walk in Spirit keeping your eyes, mind and heart on HIM. You have one Life….One love… One Spirit…. Every moment is a choice… You have free will, what do you want to do with it?

You have to begin to train your mind to control your thoughts, keep your eyes on Christ and you can achieve your goals. You must train your mouth to create your world, because what you think dictates what you say and what you say creates your life. You have the power to walk this world as Christ did and to work the miracles He did. That is what He wants you to do. If you have begun to monitor your thoughts you should begin to see a pattern in your life. Are you going in circles, dwelling on the same things over and over? Once you begin to change your habitual thinking and focus your thoughts you should see your attitude improving.

We are not in this wonderful mission alone; each of us has guides, guardians and teachers who the Lord has

A New Age of God

appointed to help you. They exist to help you to achieve your purpose and grow closer to a God centered life.

Paying attention is vital to your connection with the Holy Spirit. You must be watchful and listen at all times. Lives are wasted sleepwalking as in a trance, hypnotized by the monotony and routine of your life. You were not designed to be asleep at the wheel of your life. You must strive to remain awake. Miracles and wonders are happening every day. We are created for a purpose, but we must agree to follow that path or we wouldn't have free will. We must connect with that guidance if we are to live in Spirit. The Holy Spirit opens doors of opportunity every day and you must be aware to sense them.

Money is the tool of the enemy and the things of the world has become the focus of the masses and keeps them blinded by its imitation glitter. All that glitters is not gold and satanic distractions become satanic attractions leading you away into darkness. Money and things are not the center of the world they are a side benefit of faith. You do the work on your mind and focus and God will provide.

Is the enemy using money to keep you in bondage chasing useless things? Buy now and pay forever! You become slaves to your possessions. Once you buy the new thing that you need to be happy and the glitter fades, a newer model comes out and you are stuck with the old model while everyone is buying the latest and greatest. You are stuck dissatisfied once again on the easy payment plan. Are you going to allow your identity to be tied to that thing? Have you placed your value on your image?

No one cares that you are lying awake trying to figure out how you are going to pay for it and they call it easy financing. If you have a credit card you should be able to pay it off every 30 days; if you cannot pay it off in 30 days then put in away and pay it off in the next 30 days; if you

A New Age of God

cannot pay it off then you should cut it up and pay it off as soon as you can. You need to strive to be debt free, with the only exception of an affordable mortgage. You can manifest all you want debt free and live an affluent life if you want it.

You can have all the things you desire, but that is a side result of your life in Christ. You do not need to take an oath of poverty or sacrifice your life; Jesus wants you to be prosperous and happy. We worship a God of prosperity and abundance. You need to give 10% of what you make to God, and a minimum of 10% to yourself in savings and live on the balance, you need a backup savings to allow us to support our families for a minimum of 6 months preferably for a year. A life lived with God provides more joy and wealth than you can imagine.

Have you become a slave to your possessions that were bought to make you happy? You must be aware that the enemy uses the drive to own to work the ego and to keep you in bondage. The ego tells us we need a new car, a bigger house, a designer handbag or $300 shoes, the list could go on forever. Get sick or lose your job and where are you. You wind up at 3 in the morning wondering how you will survive the day and lay there asking God why he did this to you. I once lived in dread of the phone ringing and scared of picking up the mail. Well God didn't do that to me and He didn't do it to you, I laid down the credit card; I took the loan out on that big house and the new truck.

The enemy has long term plans to keep you distracted and in bondage. The goal is to keep you believing that this is all there is, what you have is who you are so you will just keep on keeping on. Let the TV pacify you and keep you hypnotized. They tell you their version of the news, feeding you negative information. They tell you what you need, new car, bigger house, or the latest electronic gadget.

Work till you drop and let pills and alcohol help you relax because no one understands the pressures are under, after all you deserve something for all your hard work! You deserve some entertainment, you need something to help you relax and so you miss church, it's no big deal, after all the big game is coming on and it's the playoffs or the kids have a game this Sunday. The weekend is my only time for me and Sunday I need to be with the kids and get ready for Monday. The excuses can go on forever!

What does it teach the kids when you rationalize why church isn't that important? Who is in charge of your life? How are you doing swimming upstream all alone?

HOW MUCH HAPPINESS ARE YOU GETTING FROM WHAT YOU ARE DOING NOW?

How happy are you on a daily basis? Money will rule you unless you learn to follow the spiritual laws of finance. Money cannot mean more than God! Anything that comes before you and God becomes a false idol... work...sports... partying...whatever it is, you cannot let it come before God.

>Once you stop worshiping money...

>Once you stop worshipping yourself above others...

>Once you stop worshipping the television or whatever it is that hold you back...

You will find you are much more content in your faith. The pleasures of this world will keep you in their bonds unless you make the break. Your conscious mind will fight the ways of the spirit and try to bring you back into your old comfortable routines. The goal is to keep you asleep and comfortable. Jump out of your comfort zone and find some freedom from bondage. Progress is found outside of your comfort zone!

Job 13:15. *Though He slay me...I will trust in HIM*

Job was a righteous man in the eyes of God but somehow he fell under the attack of the enemy. He lost his family and his home and he felt he was being abandoned by God. Do you feel like you have ever been persecuted in the past? Did you blame God for your problems? Job was known for his unceasing love for God. There was a tremendous price to be paid for his reputation as a man of God. If the enemy could bring down Job it would be a great victory against God.

When Job cried out to God, the Lord dispatched angels to his aid but there was such determination by the enemy for Job to fall that there was a literal war fought on his behalf. Job suffered until the war was waged and won. All this time Job was single minded in his faith, nothing could divert his faith and overshadow his relationship with God. Job stood steadfast in his faith and instead of being an example of failure he is famous for his tremendous faith.

If you are single minded in your quest for a renewed relationship with God, then you can free your mind to focus your mind on what is the true reality of your life. You are a spirit being in an earthly body. You must strive to operate in the spirit or you are living a half-life. You are the walking dead if you don't operate as a spirit filled person. You must find your faith!

A New Age of God

The Game of Life

How are you scoring in life?

What do you think your life stats are? Do you love sports? Do you arrive at home horse from yelling for your team? Do you devote the same love and enthusiasm for God? Are you really giving your all for God's team?

There is a greater game afoot in which you are the captain of your team. If you have children, are you teaching them what is important? What are your priorities? Do you stare at the TV and hide from the world, including your family? Take a few minutes and honestly assess how you think you score in your game of life. When do you do you teach your family about prayer and praise, the two most important things in your relationship with God. Our children learn by how we live and what we say. They are a living witness for your life. This is not a joke or diversion:

> It is a game of life or death
>
> Life is not a trivia contest
>
> Are you living a trivial life?
>
> When you face the throne for judgment you are faced to look upon your life and give witness to your life's work Jesus won't care who won or who scored!
>
> He won't care how many stats you know
>
> He will know your stats!!!!
>
> He knows how you played the ultimate game.
>
> You are participating in the greatest game around

A New Age of God

How are you scoring in the game of life?

How much time do you spend on God?

Choose Life: Living in the Spirit or Choose death: living in the flesh

It's time to wake up!!! He died for you...Jesus came here to show you how to live. He suffered the sins of the world on that cross to allow you salvation.

Have you considered what Jesus went through for you?

What are you doing with that great sacrifice? Don't fail to see your path. Change your mind about your life and change your life. Join those who God is calling to make a better world. Try being of this world but not in this world. When you are of the world you can be a spectator and stay apart from the fray. When you are in the world you are in the middle of it all and you are not able to observe with clear vision what is really going on. When you stay above it all they are unable to hypnotize you into following the masses.

CHAPTER 6

Forgiveness

2 Chronicles 7:14. *If my people, which are called by my name, shall humble themselves, and pray, and seek my face, turn away from their wicked ways; then I will hear from heaven, and will forgive their sin and heal their land.*

It is time for you to heal; it's time to take your pain and lay it at the foot of the cross. Carrying hurt and resentment will destroy your life and you won't be able to see the good that surrounds your life. Once you give the pain and the hurt in your life to Jesus it is like dropping an anchor you have been dragging behind you. God's love is unconditional and by his grace we are saved. Through his forgiveness we are healed of our sins and become a new person. It doesn't matter what you have done there is forgiveness awaiting you.

You can clear the past, you can be forgiven and you can forgive yourself. If you have been hurt in the past, you do not have to carry that burden alone, there is someone who wants to take that pain from you and heal your heart. Lay your pain down, give it away, forgive those that hurt you and allow yourself to be forgiven. When you accept salvation through the grace of Christ you must also allow yourself to be forgiven. This means you are a new person in Christ and your slate has been washed clean before the Lord and it becomes day one of your new life.

That means you will have to let yourself off the hook and let it all go. You have asked for the Lord to bless you and accepting grace means blessing yourself too. The worse your history the greater the testimony you will be when you begin living for the glory and love of the Father. The hardest criminal can be saved, the drug addict can be cured in an instant and whatever burden that you are carrying can be given it away. You can clear the past, and you can forgive yourself. We all have been hurt in the past, but we do not have to carry that burden alone any longer, there is someone who wants to take that pain from you and heal your heart. Lay your pain down and give it away, forgive those who have hurt you, forgive yourself for past mistakes, and allow yourself to be forgiven. Even the hardest criminal in prison has crumbled into tears when they finally realize they can have forgiveness.

Forgiveness was the pivotal step in my journey to receiving the Holy Spirit. Since the day I let it all go I have never been the same, there is a joy that fills my heart every day. I give thanks to my Lord and Savior for giving me a real life and not the cheap imitation I was living before. In the past my mantra was I don't think I can do this every moment was a struggle. Every day I walked with a lead lining around my heart. Now my heart is open and I see endless possibilities on my horizon; I am free!

You must guard your mind and your heart because they set the boundaries of your life. God is constantly trying to

A New Age of God

expand your boundaries and your comfort zone. You have to accept ownership of your inheritance from the Father.

If you hold on to the past it will haunt you and hold you back from your future. You can try to make amends but eventually you must move on. Think of it as taking a shower and putting on clean clothes. You are washing away the past soil of yesterday and you are donning a new spiritual set of clothes. As you clear away the past you are allowing yourself to grow in the present. If you don't know what's holding you back then it is time to ask for help.

With each meditation and prayer session begin with a request for guidance from God and to be shown what you need. Take an honest look at your life and see if you have any buried trauma that you are harboring. Take a serious inventory of all the wrongs you have suffered and all the wrongs you have committed. Admit your mistakes and ask forgiveness and leave them in the past. If you harbor any ill will let it go and let God worry about the retribution. As you progress you will be shown more and more of what you need to clear up and you will literally feel lighter afterwards.

There is something called cellular memory that anyone who has suffered trauma has stored up within the body. The cells store the trauma that you experienced, especially the heart, it holds that pain and damage within the cellular structure. There is only one way to clear up that damage and that is through healing prayer and forgiveness. Each time you relive a bad experience the mind takes you back in time to relive that experience again and you are traumatized again and more damage is done. The only way to heal is through forgiveness, prayer and giving it to God. When you give it away it can no longer hurt you and you can heal and be free.

A New Age of God

People with eating disorders are trying to maintain their safety by using food either for comfort, love or to isolate themselves as punishment for perceived wrongs. Cutting and hurting themselves such as pulling out their hair they are trying to release their trauma that is stored within. Only through forgiveness and release can the issue be addressed at the spiritual level. The obese person is trying to insulate themselves from the hurt they think the world holds for them. I know I avoided uncomfortable things by keeping myself insulated with fat when I weighed 300lbs.

I pray that each individual who seeks change that they will be able to achieve all you possibly can. There are basic steps to clearing the past, clearing the connection to the Spirit and developing the light within.

You need to find a bible based church that makes you feel welcome and loved. It is essential to find a spiritual leader that you can connect with. I recommend you find a nondenominational church that will accept you for who you are. This is the place where they can join you in agreement for the Holy Spirit to help you clear the past and genuinely help you receive forgiveness so you may live under grace and you can forgive yourself and move on with your life. It is essential for all believers to find salvation through Jesus Christ. Everyone needs a spiritual guide to help them find their way. We are not intended to make this journey alone!

> **Acts 2:38.** *Then Peter said unto them, repent, and is baptized every one of you in the name of Jesus Christ for the remission of sins, and you shall receive the Holy Ghost.*

A New Age of God

Tell Jesus you have lived long enough without Him in your life. Ask Jesus to forgive your past mistakes and allow yourself to be forgiven.

If you haven't been baptized by being totally immersed in water in the name of Jesus then speak with your Pastor and get yourself baptized. It is essential to be washed clean in the name of Jesus.

The next step is to seek the Holy Spirit. The Holy Spirit is a gift of the Lord and there is no way to earn or prove you are worthy of this great gift. It is more like a state of mind or alignment that you come into. First thing is to ask for help from the Holy Spirit, your guides, guardians and teachers to understand your purpose. Thank God for all He has done for you. The next step is to Say this prayer out loud with emotion and belief:

Heavenly Father I accept and believe that Jesus died on the cross and was reborn. I know Jesus accepted the sins of the world so that we can be saved. Jesus tore the Holy Veil to allow us access to the Holy Spirit and be forgiven of our sins. I accept Jesus as my Lord and Savior. I ask for Your help so I may be reborn in Spirit so that I may walk closer in your will. I ask that I be granted the gift of the Holy Spirit into my life. I ask Jesus to become the center of my life and intercede for me on the mercy seat. I believe that you and only you can change me and remake me into the person YOU want me to be. In Jesus name I ask for you to come into my life. Amen

Take an inventory of how you spend your days; do an honest evaluation of how you lead your life. Decide what needs to change and start to make small changes in the way you spend your time. God requires you to be faithful and you cannot put things before him. Start you day with God every day. I am asking you to devote 30 to 45 minutes of your morning to God. Do this every day for

A New Age of God

30 days and you will be amazed at the difference it will make in your life.

Pray out loud...baby Christians usually begin their prayer life asking for what they want and negotiating with God. Please do not waste your time negotiating for what you think you need. God already knows what you need and is ready to provide. This is not the purpose of prayer; you are seeking the Holy Spirit to lead you in your life. Spend the first 10 minutes of your day praying, praising and seeking the guidance you will need for your day. Learn to be quiet and listen as part of this prayer time. You can't have a two way conversation if you don't listen for a response. It may come as an inspiration, an impulse or a revelation. You must monitor your feelings; don't let the message slip by.

Read the Word everyday out loud for a minimum of 10 minutes. Reading out loud is essential; your mind believes what it hears you say. Each you speak Godly words you are teaching your mind to think Godly thoughts. You need to read the word of God to get your mindset for the day.

Do a 10 minute meditation with your focus on what direction you need in your life. Your heart will guide you in what you need. At the end of your session take a minute to visualize you day, see yourself going through your day, accomplishing everything you want and being a part of the body of Christ. Ask that God open your mind so you might understand, open your eyes so may see the miracles of this life and open your heart so you may love. Guide your mouth so you may only be a positive force. If you follow this routine, you will see a tremendous change in your attitude and your life. Give this a 30 day trial and be amaze

I want you to understand that forgiveness is the thing that separates us from other religions. We are the ones

A New Age of God

who worship a forgiving God that allows us to move on from the past and move forth in love. The greatest commandment that Jesus put forth was to do love you neighbor as you love yourself.. God will forgive you anything, if you will come to Him with a contrite heart and truly ask and believe you will be forgiven.

In most cases it is easier to forgive those that have wronged us than it is to forgive ourselves; especially if you are one of those people that take ownership of everything around you and find a way to make it your fault. That is what I call suffering from the "if only'"; if only I had done this thing or that thing I could have prevented the whole thing. Never, ever take responsibility or ownership of something that isn't yours.

If your one of these people, welcome to my world. For years everything that happened was my fault. I drove a truck long haul for close to 20 years and we would be on the road for four to six weeks at a time. I was devoted to providing for my grandchildren so they could have the things they wanted and their parents could not afford. I thought that was my job to provide for them to help appease the regret I suffered for giving up my children. It wasn't that I was trying to buy their love; it was just that I could do something that I was unable to do as a teenager.

I watched my daughter go in and out of abusive relationships, sell her food stamps for drugs and let her children go hungry. I stood idly by and allowed all these things to happen when my grandchildren were babies. Finally she lost custody of her 3 boys and it seemed to be a wake-up call for her.

She moved to a new city with her baby daughter who was just an infant and attempted to start over. She met a nice man who seemed to love them very much. He made good money and seemed to be a good husband and a loving Father to my granddaughter. Turned out he was

A New Age of God

on drugs and was a pedophile. He molested my sweet granddaughter from age 3 to age 12.

I took ownership of the fact that once again because I wasn't there except for visits something horrible happened. If only I had been there I could have stopped or prevented it. I had never wanted to kill anyone with my bare hands before but because of this I was ready to kill.

I was racked with a hatred that consumed me. Guild ravaged me as I went over and over what I should have done; what I should have seen...on and on it went. The abuser was arrested and through the trial I supported my daughter with unconditional love and compassion and did all that I could to help. This thing ate at my family like a cancer and has eventually finished off the fragile relationship I had with my daughter.

I love them all with all my heart and I wish I could fix it all and make the past go away for them. God in His mercy did not give those powers to me. All He could do was hold me up and keep me from killing someone. I went years trying to cope with the hatred I had for this man and the damage he did to my little girl.

I forgave everyone in my life for anything they might have done to me or because of me. I took it all to the cross and laid it at Jesus feet and asked Him to handle it for me. I ask Him to forgive everyone for what they had done and not to let anyone be punished because of what I might have done. I forgave everyone except deep down I still hated 2 people; the molester (who is serving his sentence in prison) and myself!

I wanted God to put His vengeance on this man and never allow him to hurt another child and I couldn't understand how God could have allowed this to happen to my baby girl. She was the center of my universe and I couldn't fix it and God didn't protect her. On and on the rampage

A New Age of God

went on inside, every time I thought I had it under control it would resurface and off I would go again. I wanted Old Testament revenge and nothing happened. Every day the sun came up and I drug my feet through the day, wondering why all this happened.

Satan can wreck you ideal life if the people around you open the door for him. Here I was trying so hard to get closer to God and live the life He was calling me to live. I wasn't making any progress, my prayers felt like they were falling into thin air, and I was feeling more and more separated from God every day. Daily I would cry out to God for help and I was beginning to feel like this was just something I had to bear for the rest of my life. God had told me to move to Lubbock Texas to start my life for God. My first reaction was Lubbock? Why did I need to move away to West Texas to serve God? I fought it as long as I could, until one day I surrendered and moved.

My nephew invited me to this little church that a friend had introduced him to. I was skeptical because I had some bad experiences with church but I decided to go just to make him happy. The first time I thought it was interesting but not really for me. I had never been to a spirit filled church but the Pastor was so open and unique that I was intrigued. It took about four trips and all of a sudden I was spending the service in tears but I had no idea what was happening to me. It was something I had never experienced; the Holy Spirit was touching my heart and breaking down all those walls I had worked to put up.

One Sunday we had a guest Pastor, Randy Shankle from North Carolina this man has the gift of discerning what you are going through and what you need. I have no idea what the original plan was for his sermon but when he started to speak he changed his mind and he talked about the gift of forgiveness and the power it has in our

A New Age of God

lives. He said if we are to move into a closer relationship with God then we must be ready to forgive ourselves for our mistakes and for the things that we had neglected to do in our lives. It hit me like a lightning bolt that I hated myself for mistakes I had made between the ages of 15 and 19. I hated myself for not being a mother to my kids. I hated myself because I had allowed my grandchildren to be hurt and did nothing. I hated myself for "allowing" the molester to get into my family. I had drank and did drugs because I got lost and couldn't find my way out; now I was 59 years old and still I hated myself!

Almost in a trance I walked up for a prayer and I asked for help to lay all this down and find some peace. I felt I was not worthy of forgiveness, but being worthy does not enter into the equation. Jesus loves me unconditionally and I was just a lost child coming home. Imagine the weight of the world sitting on your shoulders and it lifting off your shoulders and after decades of pain it was gone! It was a miracle just made for me. The feeling of releasing all this pain after all those years was indescribable. Forty years of flogging myself every day and keeping up a front for my husband and the rest of the world.

The next step was the molester! I had to let that go somehow. I prayed and prayed asking God for a solution so my heart could finally heal. (A quick footnote: never ask God what to do unless you are willing to do what He says). God spoke to me and told me I had to write him a letter telling him that I forgave him for destroying my family and hurting my baby girl, I had to buy him a bible and send it to the prison. That was the hardest letter I ever had to write (it took me three weeks to write it, but as I wrote I felt the pain and anger start to lift and I actually began to feel a peace come into my being. Next I had to find the prison and find out how to send it to him. The whole thing took about a month.

A New Age of God

No matter what it is that you have been holding onto God can heal you. This was the pivotal step to my growing in Christ and opening my heart to the Holy Spirit. Since that day I have never been the same, there is a joy that fills my heart every morning. Each day I ask to be refilled and I give praise and thanks to my Lord and Savior for the amazing life I now have.

Once you have been forgiven and you want to begin to remake yourself in a new image with a new life you are going to have to leave the past behind you. When you hold a grudge you are constantly replaying those events in your mind. Every time you think about those harmful things you are taking yourself back and reliving it all over again. These replays continue to harm you and keep you trapped in the past.

People have a tendency to dwell either in a pool of regret or feed the flame of self-righteous indignation. The biggest lament most people have is," Why did that happen to me?" What it all comes down to is this; what about me? They get lost in a pool of emotion; replaying everything over and over. The mind works to keep you trapped in the past events. It doesn't matter what has happened to you, regardless of how bad; it's what you do after the event that matter. Hate is the weapon of the enemy that keeps you separated from your life and worse of all it separates you from your spiritual self and God. Once you are forgiven you must release those thoughts and free your mind from the past.

It doesn't matter what you did yesterday, what matters is what you do today and how you live right now at this moment. You build your life one moment at a time, one thought at a time and you are creating what you will be tomorrow. Don't you want to be a happier person tomorrow than you were today? You do not have to stand in judgment about anything that has occurred; you can

A New Age of God

give it over to the greatest judge of all and allow God to take care of it all. We as Christians must be known for our love and compassion. Every action is a direct reflection on the Savior and we must make an effort to live in His image. We all must us the same care and love with ourselves as we do others.

Forgiveness heals us and frees us to live in the moment and to create the world we want to live in. You are not a prisoner of the past, but a resident of the present. God allows us to decide who we want to be, and gives us the power to create our own world.

If you have tried and failed to move forward stop and consider if the past is keeping you in guilt and conviction. To live in the present and to create your future you must allow Jesus to wipe your slate clean and move on. We must be like Paul when he left Saul behind on the Damascus road.

> **Psalm 51:1-2.** *Have mercy upon me, O God, according to thy loving kindness: according unto the multitude of your tender mercies blot out my transgressions. Wash me thoroughly from my inequities and cleanse me from my sin.*

CHAPTER 7

Purpose

The carnal is a person led by his senses and his emotions. Spirit filled is when we learn to operate in the spirit we are led by God through the direction of the Holy Spirit. Once we decide to ignore the carnal impulses and we accept that we are Spiritual beings in earthly form; then we begin to see how we have been seduced by the world to accept what we see in the world and to ignore our Spirit life. Our logical mind wants us to put this all aside and get on with our lives; after all as hard as we work don't we deserve a little entertainment, so just sit down and relax, tune in the TV and tune out our minds.

Living a Spirit filled life is the goal, to achieve this we should learn we are not our emotions and feelings; put aside the distractions and make space for your spiritual work so you may start to feed your Spirit and allow it to grow. Your Spirit needs to be fed by the Holy Spirit so it may blossom through the connection with God.

Time is a manmade illusion which came into being when Adam lost his spiritual essence. Satan's mission relies on time because he operates on the earthly plane. That is why he wants you kept in time so he can keep you in dominion. Once you realize time is an illusion you can

A New Age of God

then begin to operate in the supernatural. This world is an illusion and everything that is here was first created in heaven and manifested on the earth.

> **John 3:5-8.** *Verily, verily I say unto thee, except a man is born of water and of the Holy Spirit, he cannot enter into the kingdom of GOD. That which is born of the flesh is flesh; and all that is born of the Spirit is Spirit. Marvel not that I said unto you, you must be born again.*

Don't let the term born again put you off. Different connotations have been associated with the experience. Being born again is deeply personal and spiritual achievement that is different for each individual. If you want to find your spiritual purpose and receive your gifts you need to accept Jesus as your Lord and Savior. You must accept the word of God and realize that God is the one source and look to Him in all things.

You cannot earn it or deserve it, but the key to receiving the Holy Spirit is to ask. It is the greatest gift that the Ultimate Power can give you while we walk the earth. It is sought through sincere, heartfelt prayers (out Loud) and praises to receive the filling of the Holy Spirit. You can't earn it; you can't buy it. All you need is a sincere desire to receive. You cannot conceptualize the Holy Spirit with the conscious mind, you can't find it through intellect, you can only open yourself to God's will and allow. Stop searching with your mind and open up your heart in faith. Without an open heart and expectancy you will not receive.

There is an anxiety that precedes all spiritual evolution and it is completely normal. You will feel like something is about happen but you have no idea what is happening to

A New Age of God

you. It feels like a quaking of the spirit. This is the normal evolution of the awakening of the spiritual side.

When I was working towards alignment with the spirit so I could receive the Holy Spirit I read Psalm 51 three times a day out loud. Within 2 weeks I could tell the changes that were happening within. I began to grow a better attitude and it helped me keep my eyes on God. It speaks of being remade, David was rejoicing over his broken bones so that He might be remade, of being washed white as snow.

This process takes you out of your comfort zone because you are stepping up in faith and will change your life. Anytime you do something new the mind tries to stop you and make you go back to your old routine. The mind only wants to do what it has always done because that is known territory and it is safe and comfortable.

When you are transcending to a new level of consciousness you are being altered spiritually and you will have to go past the anxiety and emotion to stay on your path. You are in the process of being remade to achieve a new alignment with the Father. It is a purifying that cleanses out the old ways and replaces it with a new more spiritual self. Every time you pray, praise and meditate you are focusing your mind on God. Every time you read the word out loud you are building your faith, for what the mouth says the mind believes.

You are working within to accept the power of God. Gradually you will change your wayward conscious mind and evolve into a new way of thinking and seeing the world. The further you go into this new life in Jesus the more you come into alignment and move one step closer to the essence of man that the creator intended for each of us. Jesus operated in the supernatural and He wants you to assume your inheritance and claim the power he

A New Age of God

died to give you. God has great plans and expectations for you. He wants you to live a life of abundance and joy.

There comes a time of connection when for a moment you will experience a glimpse of the universe that lies within. There is a universe that lives between each breath, between each heartbeat. That is where God lives within waiting for you to take a step in faith to reach for Him.

> **Acts 2:17.** *And it shall come to pass in the last days, said God; I will pour out my Spirit upon all flesh: and your sons and your daughters shall prophecy, and your young men shall see visions, and your old men shall dream dreams. And on my servants and on my handmaidens I will pour out in those days my Spirit; and they shall prophecy.*

Most of the modern church either does not believe in receiving the Holy Spirit, they believe it is just a metaphor for finding God in the Bible. They feel that when you are baptized you automatically receive the Holy Spirit (and some people do but not everyone). In my experience, what I have been taught and from what I have read in the New Testament it is a separate event that cements a coming into alignment with God.

The Holy Spirit bypasses the logical mind, so you must disengage you logic and receive in faith. The Holy Spirit is a filling up of the void that waits within. Truth is the mouth of the Father and His tongue is the Holy Spirit. When you are blessed with the Holy Spirit it is an act of truth.

You must live in faith and truth or the Holy Spirit will depart from you. I cannot imagine the feeling of loss and emptiness if I were to lose my relationship with the Holy

A New Age of God

Spirit. It would be like living without sight or hearing and trying to live on.

You cannot analyze or try to maintain control. You must be willing to submit to a higher power to become one with the higher power. The mind will try to analyze and therefore block your progress. If you do not bypass the logic you will not be able to receive. The fact that you think you are in control is an illusion planted by this imaginary world. We live an illusion every day of our lives and the only way to wake up to reality is to learn to see the real world for what it truly is. God's creation went from the beginning to the end of time. God has already created in Heaven what we need here on Earth. You can manifest all that is Heaven to Earth if you operate in the spirit realm. Let us agree to bring down Heaven to Earth.

The enemy wants you to be selfish and only mindful of yourself. We all submit to a higher authority at some point so why not allow God to be your authority in all things. Walking alone is to live in darkness, why not walk in the light. God is willing to light your path and guide you to your purpose.

Our job is to believe God and to go back to trusting in the Lord. We must eliminate all other sources; God is the one source…Look to Him! When you work within the direction of the Holy Spirit you start to work in partnership with God. We should get our direction and purpose from the Holy Spirit and manifest our life through the Word.

When I received the Holy Spirit I had a momentary knowing and understanding of the universe and the omnipotent force which resides within the God realm. I cannot translate what it was like, only it was the most empowering and joyous experience. Each day I pray to Jesus that He will walk with me through my day and that I be refilled with the Holy Spirit. With each prayer I get a deeper and closer relationship with God. I no longer walk alone seeking a God from above but I walk each day with His precious Holy Spirit dwelling within.

In the beginning my faith was like a small bud of a rose but it has blossomed in to a beautiful radiant flower that grows on an intertwining vine that strives to grow on the cross. I have made a covenant with God that cannot be broken by man and will do His will in all that I do. There are no words in the languages of man to convey the love I feel, there can be no description of the relationship and it makes me understand the old writings of the Saints when they spoke of the ecstasy of God. I desperately want all of the seekers of God to have the relationship they're meant to have in their lives. I want us to be a shining example of His light, living in harmony with each other, with respect for one another and full of His universal love.

There are many gifts that may come to you after you receive the Holy Spirit but the one most important gift is the Holy Spirit Himself. Once you receive you will be blesses with an inner voice that will aid you as much as you allow. God never forces anyone to do anything but once you make a covenant you are responsible to fulfill that promise. It is possible to lose the Holy Spirit if you are not faithful in worship; if you walk away from God He will let you go.

1 Corinthians 12:4-11. *Now there are diversities of gifts (of the Holy Spirit), but of the same Spirit. And there are differences of administration, but of the same Lord. And there are diversities of operations but it is the same GOD that works all in all. But the manifestation of the Spirit is given to every man to profit withal.*

For one is given by the Spirit of the word of wisdom... To another is given the word of knowledge...

A New Age of God

> *to another is given Faith...To another the gifts of healing are given...To another the working of miracles...To another prophecy...To another the discerning of spirits...Toanother diverse kinds of tongues...To another the interpretation of tongues.*
>
> *But all these work of that same self-same Spirit, dividing to every man severally as he will.*

Once you have been blessed with the Holy Spirit there are gifts that will be designated for you that are suited for your work. What you receive depends on your purpose. We are born with the exact talents and abilities to follow our chosen predestined purpose and God will provide you with the gifts that are suited to you. Meditate and pray for the gifts you need. You will gradually come to understand your purpose and have the gifts God has blessed you with to accomplish all the goals you want to receive. You were created perfectly with the intelligence and talents to achieve your purpose. There is no time in the spirit realm and all that you need is waiting on you to claim it and take ownership of your purpose.

> **Matthew 16:25.** *For whosoever will save his life shall lose it: and whosoever will lose his life for my sake shall find it.*

Don't live this life just doing time and ignoring your true life work. Don't waste your precious life on useless things and let the important stuff slip by. You want to look back and see what you have accomplished with pride and satisfaction.

A New Age of God

One afternoon I was talking with my 70 year old mother-in-law about things in general and she said," You know now that I look back on all the things I have done in my life, I realize that what I felt were so important was really just silly things that I thought made me feel important. I worked for 35 years and I was a big success in club work. I remember when I finally bought myself a mink coat, I was so proud of myself. How many times did I put my work and club life in front of my family and my son? I could not count the times I missed ball games or even being able to be there for him at dinner or on the weekends. All I ever wanted was a child and my biggest failure was at being a Mother to my adopted son and I cannot make up for that. I just made so many mistakes that I can't fix."

She had to live with the choices she made and live with the consequences. She was a single Mom and she put her wants and needs before everything else and all her son got was the left overs. I thank God he had his Grandmother and Grandfather to show him what love was and gave him some semblance of a loving family life.

I believe the Lord sent my husband his precious grandparents to help him know the unconditional love of a family. They are the substance that he used to become a man.

Each and every human being at the end of this life has to face the life they have led. You will have a complete knowledge of God and man and when you walk to the Throne of God the path you take will be paved with all the love and the works you have done during your stay on this Earth. When you approach the Throne and face the Book of Life and you stand face to face with the Lord, how glorious will your experience be? What will you have done? What will the Lord see recorded in that Holy Book when you stand before the works of your life? This

A New Age of God

lifetime is but a speck of time in the universe and you will be facing all eternity.

You are building your next life right here and now. Regardless of your choices you have one life eternal. There is no death; you transcend this life into your true self in God. What life do you want to live through eternity?

What you do now must be done as if the Savior were physically there with you, for you know that He is with you always...Keep in mind you never walk alone. You have guardians, guides and teachers; Angels of God that have dedicated their existence to being there to help and guide you.

You are the creation of the Almighty created perfectly for your purpose; a product of God's love. You are predestined by God to be a person created out of love, a part of the plan of the Eternal one, and you are made to be Gods representative on Earth. God gave man dominion on the Earth so we could make this world as it is in Heaven.

> **Matthew 16:19** *And I will give you the keys of the kingdom of heaven: and whatsoever you will bind on Earth shall be bound in Heaven: and whatsoever you loose on Earth shall be loosed in heaven.*

The word of God is our daily bread and the Son of God came and walked this Earth; all He did was done to show you how to live. He is our salvation and he will guide you away from temptation and keep you safe from the evil of the enemy. All His sacrifice suffering was endured so that you could see your possibilities and guide you to what YOU can do right here and right now. How much vision do you have for your life? You future is unlimited!

A New Age of God

Once you submit to God, the Holy Spirit will start to guide you on your path. Your intuition will begin to grow stronger. You will need to pray for the Holy Spirit to awaken your gifts that will allow you to fulfill your purpose.

You have been a spirit being for all eternity and you choose a specific purpose that you wanted to fulfill in human form and you asked to be born. We choose what we will accomplish while we are here. Your specific gifts are for this purpose so you will have the abilities you need. You were perfectly made for who you are and endowed with talents and abilities like no one else. This is not ego; it is respecting and believing the works of God. You are wasting your time envying others for their gifts and abilities, because you must love and accept yourself for who you are.

Consider making a covenant with God to be given your purpose so you may fulfill His will. Do not do this lightly because when you make a contract with God it is not to be taken casually and there is no escape clause. There is something about making a commitment on how to live your life that makes every day a little brighter and everyday an adventure. You will no longer live in your own little world, but you will be carrying a torch for God; never to walk alone again.

Finding your purpose focuses your life and you start to live with intent. My purpose is to start a ripple effect that just might get people focused on a discussion of the state of the world, how we perceive it and of the Holy Spirit and how it relates to the world today. Think about it, if it took God one day to create the universe, then just how long is one day on earth to God. One day on earth is not even a blink of time in Heaven. How much time do you and I have to do our work?

A New Age of God

The Fact of God

The I Am of the universe is God and He is the reason for everything. The I Am resides within, communicates and exists through the Holy Spirit. Just as the stars in the sky exist, so does HE exist and HE permeates the entire universe which HE created.

If you are to succeed in achieving your purpose you will have to make some changes that are not very easy. You will have to live with intent and select what you do with your time. You will see a shift in your priorities and in the perception of the world around you. You will learn to value how you spend your time and who you spend it with. These changes are critical to your success in finding and achieving your purpose. I remember listening to the song, Is That All There Is, and hearing the lyric:

'If that's all there is to life, then let's keep dancing and break out the booze and have a ball.' If that's all there is, how many people feel that way about their life?

I just keep wondering how many people live their life like that song as if there is nothing else in life. If so that explains the sales of antidepressants in our society! What a sad commentary to think we are just putting one foot in front of the other living for the next party or ball game. If you don't want to live that way then it is time to make some choices, some small and some not so easy.

Have you ever grown a beautiful rose bush? If you have then you know if you want beautiful full blossoms you have to care for and feed the bush. The roses are the fruit of the bush and it needs the right balance of light, water and food to flourish. The nature of the rose bush is to produce as many buds as possible because that is how it reproduces. The problem is that to feed all those baby flowers it takes all its energy and his diminishes the size and quality of all the roses on the bush. They will not be as large and colorful because the bush is using all its resources to feed the buds.

If you want a beautiful full rose bush with large healthy roses you must study the bush and visualize what you want the bush to grow into. You must decide which branches you need to trim and what blooms you want to leave. Then you lovingly prune the bush into the shape you want it to be. Next you want to pinch off the excess buds so you have the number of blossoms you want. The rose bush needs to be guided to put its energy into to doing its best work. In the end you will have a beautiful, healthy plant full of luscious roses.

This analogy is the same as your life. You need to have a vision of what you want your life to be. The clearer you vision you have of what you want the easier you will manifest your dream. You are not only influenced by the thoughts you think but you are influenced by the people you decide to surround yourself with and the activities you choose to participate in. There are only so many hours in the day and it is up to you what you accomplish. You will need to surround yourself with likeminded people to encourage you and help you on your way. In life just as in building a business you need to surround yourself with the best people who share your vision or your purpose.

Just like the rose bush you will need to trim away the excess in your life to find its true essence. It is difficult to do but it is necessary to eliminate the things that distract you from your purpose. If you have friends that criticize the new life you are trying build and they want you to keep being the same old person doing the same old things

A New Age of God

then you will have to decide if they are a distraction that is holding you back.

I have had to leave friends and relatives behind because we just didn't want the same things out of life. They wanted to keep me bogged down in the past and limit what I should or shouldn't do. Back when I did drugs and I decided I just didn't want to live that way anymore, I had to leave my druggy party friends behind and they hated me for changing.

I must be careful who I surround myself with because I have a tendency to try to save the world and I waste a lot of energy on people who are just doing time and do not really want to change their situation. I have to be very careful who I associate with because I am very emotional have the gift of sharing people's emotions and pain, therefore I get all wrapped up in their situation and allow their problems to become the monkey on my back instead of theirs. It can be very distracting and emotionally draining.

If you want to receive your gifts of the Holy Spirit and you want to grow a full spiritual life then you will have to fight old habits and routines and train yourself to have discipline. There are few things harder than change and you don't have to do it over night. It doesn't matter if it is choices about your health, your friends or your job, change is never easy. Like my Mama always said nothing worth doing right is easy but the rewards are a joy to behold. Just do your best and follow your inner guide not your old routines and you will gradually start to become the person God created you to be.

Your mind always fights change. Your friends will fight your change. You will have to keep your eyes on God. Every day read Psalm 51 morning and night if you are having a hard time with changing your inner habits. Every day when you wake up thank God for your day and

A New Age of God

ask that He guide you on your path today, that he makes you the person you are supposed to be and gives you purpose for your day. Ask that He opens your eyes so you might see, open your ears so you might hear, open your mind so you might understand and to open your heart so you may give the world the love that He gives you. Ask to be His instrument as you go through the day, that he guild your armor and surround you and your family with the blood of Jesus and guide and protect us all.

Each and every day you follow the same pattern of faith your purpose and determination things will become clearer and you will grow stronger. You will become bolder in your life because you have intent and a purpose. Soon you begin to formulate a routine that will become the person who you have envisioned yourself to be and you will start to become not the vision but the person. Once you start to live your life with the intent of living with purpose you will realize you are living the life you were created for. What greater joy can that be than to wake up every day of your life with a vision of what you want and have the ability to live that life with purpose? That is the life God wants you to live.

CHAPTER 8

Being Alive

Romans 8:1-2. *There is therefore now no condemnation to them which are in Christ Jesus, who walk not after the flesh, but after the Spirit. For the law of the Spirit, of life in Christ Jesus hath made me free from the law of sin and death.*

How would you describe your love of God? It is like asking someone to describe the air they breathe or the love you have for your family. Living life the Jesus way will give you a life full of love and purpose. No more pondering the purpose of life or questioning why you were born.

I have been told that devoting your life to God requires too much sacrifice. I will tell you what I sacrificed; I forfeited a life of drugs and alcohol, feeling unloved, inadequate, existing in a depression full of guilt and fear. I gained an unending love, peace of mind and heart, a knowing that I am good enough, I am smart enough and that I am loved beyond words. I have a purpose and I have the opportunity to help someone to find a better life. In other words I no longer have a gaping hole that yearns for a

A New Age of God

filling with things. I am content under the wings of the Lord.

My love for Him is unending and the love I give Him can never come close to the love he fills me with and makes me whole. He fills the hole in me that was un-fillable before I received the Holy Spirit. The joy fills me and almost takes my breath away. I feel as if my heart will burst. I am moved to tears and get weak in the knees. My mind becomes filled with His presence; it is as if I have tapped the universe and I can see and feel His limitless presence and power within me. I become part of His Omnipresence and I know all things are possible. For a brief moment I am one with God and I understand His will.

I keep seeking Him in all I do, He shows me possibilities and inspiration unthought-of of and I can do anything through Him. God has a covenant with each of us and we need to make a covenant with Him. My covenant with the Father of us all is to follow His direction in all aspects of my life. All that I do is for Him and I give Him the credit and the Glory for every word I write and every person I touch. His word is the purpose and I am just the messenger making a feeble attempt to pass it on as He directs me.

The experience is different for everyone but my desire, my prayer is for every person to know that one clear moment of knowing. It is a life changing moment when the Holy Spirit touches you and fills the void that exists within each of us. The void will be filled with indescribable peace…words cannot be found to relay the experience. In the ancient texts the Saints called it the ecstasy of God. Guess that's as close as you can get.

A new awareness of the possible comes when you are touched by Gods presence. All you thought was wonderful now seems small in comparison. How do you repay such

A New Age of God

love? He paid the ultimate price so that you might live the light of the Lord and salvation. You need to understand how much He loves you and how important you are in the scheme of things. You are the key to the universe and what you do matters beyond counting. If you just change the world three feet around you and you inspire someone else to do the same, start a chain reaction and then you could be responsible for changing the world. If one person touches and changes just two people for the better and the chain reaction continues it could reach around the planet.

So many times an act of careless or evil has changed someone's world and they were never the same again. One drunk driver can devastate a family or one drug dealer getting his hands on one of your children and your world is altered, never to be the same again.

Well the same is true for God, just one blessed touch and you can be altered for life and through that you could change the life of your family and friends. Most people do not think about how good changes people; all we hear about is the bad things that happen.

Once you are touched by the Holy Spirit you become one of His works on Earth. You start to be gently guided by His soft touch in all the things you do. If you stray He will convict you of your mistake so you can realize whatever it is and you can ask forgiveness. This is not done out of anger but out of love, for He wants you to be the best that you can be. You will be remade into a better more beautiful person. Whenever you feel guilty or have remorse for something you have done that is the Holy Spirit moving within you to help you see your mistakes. Your inner voice becomes stronger and more guiding as time goes by.

Watch the press and the media to discern the slant they have on people of God. They are working hard these days

A New Age of God

to keep us from believing and thinking it is old fashioned to seek God and His wisdom.

I don't know who they have been talking to, but as far as I'm concerned there is a huge need for God in this world. People have been cured of cancer, a terminal patient wakes from a coma in perfect condition and I know a teenager who had a hole in her heart that was completely healed. I have seen a manic depressive receive the Holy Spirit and never need a drug again. I met a man that was hooked on heroin and it was killing him a little more each day and God took away his addiction in an instant without withdrawal.

Don't we need miracles anymore? Is there really no time for God? It's time to wake up folks; our kids are killing themselves with drugs and alcohol. They are erasing their memories taking drugs so they can have more fun and be less inhibited when they party. Our families need structure, love and rules if we are going to have a society of human beings. I guess that is my main point; we must choose if we want to be human beings with a spiritual life or do we want to live as animals, relying solely on instinct and emotions? What kind of world do you want to build?

The work here is to make us messengers of love! We must take responsibility to stop the insanity of this world and come back to a place where there is someone more important than our selves. Our mandate from the Father of us all to make it on Earth as it is in Heaven. Love is the only way we can come back from the brink of destruction. The love of our Almighty Father is the guide. Follow the teachings of Jesus and do unto others as you want to be treated. Give someone a hand up, give them an encouraging word and you will be amazed how much better you feel about the world and yourself. Take what we have discussed and put it to work and you will change your world.

A New Age of God

I have given you the knowledge and the tools to come closer to God and bring yourself into a loving relationship with the Father of us all so that you walk in love and protection under His guidance. You have the tools to follow God and not man. You have the knowledge to have the universe as your guide.

One of my favorite people is the Reverend Jesse Duplantis and he says that religion is genetically altered Christianity and I could not agree more. Brother Jesse is one of the most joyful, inspiring people I have ever listened to. He and I see the Lord with the same eyes. Somehow the church evolved into a message of fear and retribution attempting to scare people; somewhere the message of eternal love was lost and self-righteousness took its place.

Lost is the message of the unbreakable bond that man has as Gods chosen beloved ones and how it is maintained through love and worship. Love is the key to serving in God's army. The New Age of God will bring back the joy and love to mankind.

The commandments of God were given to man so that we might have the tools we need to live in a world where Satan walks. The commandments are guidelines to keep Satan away from your life. Evil exists in the world and if you don't believe it just look around.

Take a trip to Las Vegas or any casino and look around. Sure it is supposed to be a playground to relax and have fun, but just look beyond the lights and glitter. They give you free drinks so you will sit there and give them more and more of your money, selling you the dream that you could be the next big winner. Open your eyes and look beyond the glitter and the lights; there lies in the dark the seedy side of the glamour.

Gambling, prostitution and alcohol mix in a world where anything goes. People with a limited income are giving

A New Age of God

away their money on the chance they might hit it big under the premise of having fun! Soberly walk around and watch and judge for yourself how much fun they seem to be having. There doesn't seem to be much fun on their faces. I'd rather put my trust in a sure thing, God.

Just look at the homeless wandering the streets of Las Vegas and everywhere else in our nation; most have a mental problem or drugs and alcohol has stolen their lives and they are scared, lost, hungry and cold. People say there is nothing wrong with having a drink now and then, but just look at the people who scrounge up their last few coins to put together beer money. Please go to an AA meeting and listen to the stories of what alcohol has cost them. They too would have told you they had it under control as they were spiraling out of their lives.

Watch most movies as they drag you down into a cesspool of drugs and violence. They are preying on your animal emotions to keep you in bondage, keeping you at a level where you cannot see any hope in the world. The news has made us bad news addicts reinforcing the feeling there is no hope in the world.

You are the guardians of your soul and your mind, and you have to control what you watch, what you think and what you expose you and your family to. When you allow garbage into your mind and the mind of your family in the name of entertainment you are erring and you open the door for evil and strife to enter your life.

Satan roams the Earth striving to keep man in bondage so you are separated from the Father and are walking alone at his mercy (which he has none). The commandments are there to protect you and help keep evil from slipping into your life. The enemy wants you to stumble so he can hold you down. When you ignore Gods guidelines you invite evil and harm into your life.

A New Age of God

Satan knows your weak spots; he knows what your buttons are and how to push them. You can be the best person in the world and if one of your children gets sucked into the bad influences that lurk everywhere, the enemy has a way into your life to hurt you. One boyfriend or girlfriend that has a wild side and dabbles in drugs or drinks too much can open the door for disaster. If we don't teach our children about the dangers and how they can destroy not only their life but the lives of their family we leaving them open to attack.

Satan loves to prey on the children of pastors. If the enemy can get ahold of their children then there is the possibility they can be drawn away from God or at least tormented with the judgments of others whether they are justified or not. Trust me being faithful to God and living the proper life can be a double edged sword if you don't keep your armor on and your trust and faith in God.

The better life you lead the more abhorrent you are to the enemy and he will try to pull you down to his level. Any triumph against a good Christian just makes Satan's day.

I have given you the steps to build up your relationship through praise and worship and brought you to the place where you have the armor of God to protect you. Now it is time for you to start living the life as it was intended since creation. Mankind was created to be loved above all else. Satan lives in envy of this love and seeks to separate you from what he cannot have.

If you are devout and follow God in all things but you have a child that refuses to walk in the light and that child allows evil to influence their life, they have opened the door for you to be attacked. The enemy does not follow any rules; he and his minions will destroy your family to get to you. Satan wants you to blame God for what happens to your family.

A New Age of God

Satan will work through your family, your friends and your work. He will use the media to sell your children a bill of goods that will start them in the wrong direction. Be aware of what they watch on TV, what games they play, where they go on the internet. Satan can take the most innocent thing such as a small child and turn it into a perversion. This is war my friends and you cannot go around unarmed if you want to walk in the light. We can take this world back and make it a paradise again if we just walk in the light of God together.

It is up to you to teach your children the guidelines and enable them to walk in the light. You must surround yourself with the light of protection God provides and keep your family protected. Do not invite deceit into your home and into your life. Keep your domain Holy. Your mind is your domain just as your house is. Keep yourself in the light of the cross. Jesus died so that we could have a direct relationship with the Holy Spirit. He shed His blood for you to be protected so use that blood for your protection.

There is a little voice that speaks to you 24 hours a day to keep you where you have always been and they are the voices of your mind. Most people have about 50 thoughts that just repeat themselves in a loop over and over. Most of it is ideas that were imprinted by our family, teachers and others that helped to program us when we were growing up. We base our self-image on how we have been treated and we believe what we have been told as children. Most of it seems harmless but a lot of it is negative information that we have accepted as a truth.

If you have lived with prejudice and discrimination there is a lot of anger and pain that has damaged yourself image and how you see the world. There are dirty little lies that have been planted in every one of us. These are the things that create the mindset you live with every day. The sad thing is the lies are passed down from

A New Age of God

one generation to the next and you start to expect the very thing you hate. We create our world with what we expect and what we say. The power you hold within is tremendous and it can work for or against you. The key is to change the cycle that perpetuates the lie.

You can reprogram those thoughts but it takes work. You must be conscious of what you are thinking and rebuke those thoughts that harm us or cause us doubts. Satan wants to keep you in the death and bondage of this world and he will use that small voice and your emotions to attack you. The enemy will try to convince you that nothing will ever change and that is the way it has always been.

That is why when you start to turn your mind to God and change how you think and act you will come under attack. Satan will lose his grip on you if he cannot deter your change. If he cannot stop you from changing he will resort to other means and put up obstacles to distract you.

There will come a time before you have built up your spiritual armor that you won't know how to protect yourself and the door will still be ajar to allow those thoughts to take root in your mind and Satan's minions will do their best to frighten you away. They will tell you this is all make believe or that we live in a modern age and we have evolved beyond all this God stuff.

Whatever the doubts you have harbored over the years the evil ones know too and they will use these doubts and weaknesses. Whatever frightens you they will use it to manipulate you. That is where your faith dissolves those attacks and gives you strength to keep your eyes on God.

The stronger the attack on your life the greater fear Satan has of you. It isn't much consolation that the attacks on you are a compliment on your potential, but if you reach

A New Age of God

out to God and keep your determined faith you will be able to rebuke the attack.

We have been led to believe that if we disobey God we will go to Hell but the punishment for going against the rules of life is right here on Earth. The punishment is not because God wants you to suffer, that's why He gave you the commandments so you could avoid Hell on Earth for your protection. You have free will and you have to make your own choices but you have to accept the responsibility for what you do. To live a committed life of obedience is to follow the guidelines of protection God has provided for you so you can live in the now in joy.

If you put anything before you and God you are giving the enemy a tool to use against you. Love nothing more than God. Love your spouse, love your children but do not love anything or anyone more than God. If you do you are giving an open invitation for it to a weapon to separate you.

You are living in a war zone; you must build up and wear your spiritual armor. Keep your eyes on God. Every time you thank God for something you build your shield of faith. Every time you worship and praise you build up your armor. Every time you meditate on God, he builds up your strength to keep your covenant. God does not go back on his covenants; He does not change His mind about you. You were created in love above all others and are the most treasured in the universe.

You are unique and have everything you need to live in joy. You have the responsibility to live a Godly life and lead others to the light and give them the knowledge to live a life of joy.

The Holy Spirit's sole purpose is to love and guide you on your path. He wants to be the guiding voice in your life. We are blessed with a direct connect with the Father

A New Age of God

that is there to love and guide you. We know what is expected of us and we know how to understand the rules of engagement.

All it takes is a request, just a whisper to our Almighty Father, and everything can be different. Give a little love and feel the floodgates open and let the love of God reign down on you.

A Whisper of the Infinite

A whisper can reach the infinite
That fills your inner being
A whispered request to the Father
That brings you unlimited favor
A whisper that brings the word of God alive
It opens your understanding
Of things not yet known
A whisper that bestows the gifts of the Holy Spirit
It awakens your world
A whisper that allows you to be in this world
But not be of this world
To live in contact
No longer alone
To have the Almighty as your guide
A whisper that brings the universe to my feet
A whisper to the King is all that is needed

CHAPTER 9

School of the word

Throughout this book we have emphasized the importance of the word. The power of the spoken word and the written word of God cannot be emphasized enough. Combine prayer, praise and meditation and you have the powerful tools to change your life and the lives of your family and friends. The whole thing together is intended to help you understand the workings of the Holy Spirit in your life, what God's intention is for His children and to help you achieve a balance between the mind, the body and the spirit so you have all the tools you will ever need to be led, educated and loved by God.

People around the world are starving for a taste of the one true God in their life. My intention has been to give anyone who seeks God the tools and steps that will give you the ability to reach out to God and finally get an answer.

Here in the United States we take for granted the freedom we have to worship freely regardless of faith. We need to treasure this freedom and be ready to defend this right to the death. The Father of us all is tired of His children taking their lives and purpose for granted.

A New Age of God

God should be first and foremost in your life. Christ should be the center of your life; you should have control of the mind (not the mind and the emotion controlling you), be the body of Christ and live within the spirit to lead a healthy and productive life. The first thing on your mind every morning should be God. Resolve to follow your routine of worship and keep His laws and He will protect and guide you. God will honor his covenants with man and man should make his covenants in life as well as with the Father of us all.

> **John 17:8.** *For I have given unto them the words which you gave me; and they have received, and have known surely that I came out from you, and they have believed that you did send me.*

The secret to solving any problem is to understand the root cause and then you can make the changes needed. It is time to stop making excuses for our weaknesses and see that the animal virus has spread in man like a cancer and we must understand why we are the way we are so we may overcome and kill off the virus of death that holds us in bondage. There is a cure and it lies with God. If you have something within that is in error and once you recognize it, you can then work to change things and make it acceptable in Gods eyes.

Survival of the fittest should be for the animal kingdom and nor for mankind. We are designed to be caretakers and to build Heaven on Earth. God made us in His image, to walk hand in hand with Him. We have to live with honor, learn to respect each other, and allow others to live within the dictates of their beliefs and culture. Every human being on this planet deserves to live with respect and honor. If we could learn to celebrate our differences

A New Age of God

we could learn to live in peace. Our diversity is what gives this world color and beauty.

We were given dominion on this planet which is the gem of the universe and that gives us a responsibility to be the keepers of the Earth and our fellow man. The condition of the world has been created by man and must be restored and cherished by man. The most valuable commodity on this planet is clean drinking water. We cannot live without water and clean air.

It is our responsibility to be the caretaker and we cannot ignore our part. We must start to honor ourselves, others and our planet. We must look at the impact we have with how we live and try to leave this planet in a better condition than we left it. We as a species are failing God, our planet and our families. The male was meant to lead their families and their communities. Unfortunately most men have relinquished that job and have allowed the carnal infection of man to rule their lives. More and more families are splitting up and the men are moving on and leaving their children and wife behind, and leaving her to be the leader of the family. It seems as no one wants to lead they just want to exist.

In my early years I was influenced by the feminist movement and worked for women to become empowered and liberated from the straight jacket society had placed on them. I wanted women the opportunity to work and to be paid equally. It seems now women are so busy trying to be men that being the loving caretaker and nurturer are being lost. Being a mother has become lost as some part time job and most kids are raising themselves with video games and television. We are allowing ourselves to devolve as a people of God.

There is a lot more to being an absentee father than just paying court ordered child support. There is more to being a Mother than picking the kids up from day care,

A New Age of God

picking up fast food and sitting the kids in front of the TV or a video game. In all this hectic madness who is raising the children that were so desperately wanted? When you marry you take a vow and that vow carries down to the children that they are your responsibility to love and not just an obligation to send money. Our children need to know they are loved and cherished by both parents and they need to learn the spiritual principals of living. You are their only hope of being taught how to live.

Men need to lovingly lead their families, guide them on their spiritual path and lead by example. You must lead and show your children how a father should behave and how to show the love every child needs to grow up healthy, spiritually, mentally and physically. Mothers your children need your love and need to be the center of your universe. Our children are the responsibility of the family and the community and we are failing them.

We have to put God at the center of our families and teach our children to worship and praise every day. It is time to put God back into their lives and show them the age of miracles through faith is still here.

People seem more concerned with Facebook, the internet and work than the people they love or their community. Most can tell you what the latest celebrity did on their reality show but they can't tell you one thing that is happening in their own child's life.

To be a leader you must be bold.

To be a teacher you must be taught.

To be a student you must submit to authority.

Everyone deserves a safe place to live and decent whole food to live. We cannot continue to leave it to the other guy to fix. Stand up and be courageous, don't be willing to live with the status quo. Make this a life worth living.

A New Age of God

We have a responsibility to live an honest Godly life and provide the children with what they need to grow up to be people who know their value and know the God of Creation lives within each and every person on the planet.

No one is better than anyone and we all deserve the respect and love that we expect for ourselves. Do unto others as you want to be done unto you and see the result of following the primary mandate of Christ on earth.

If you put material things ahead of your family, if you work eighty hours a week so you can drive a fifty thousand dollar car and two homes but ignore your family and community you are a failure. There is no way to replace the love you should be providing to your children. Buying them material things is not a substitute for love. You should be teaching them what is important in their lives. You have to teach the children before they are corrupted further by a society that is driven by advertisement and commercialism.

Men seem to feel that they must be in control of their emotions and their success is based on their possessions. They seem to be unable to allow God to lead them in their lives; perhaps they think it is unmanly to need God. For the life of me I don't understand the attraction of being a rock for your family. A rock is cold and hard, it has no heart and no feeling. Why would you want to model yourself after something like that?

I cannot imagine what it must be like to have that much pressure put on your shoulders and try to walk that path alone. Men live in a world that has been created that keeps them under constant pressure to provide for their families to a level advertisers have sold society and they have to work night and day just to keep up. I am amazed the men I know can still breathe and keep putting one foot in front of the other just to keep their heads above

A New Age of God

water. It's no wonder the nurturing and fathering has fallen by the wayside.

Women have to work to keep the family in the manner society has taught us we need. There is no time or energy to cook, and take care of the kids, so we have kids raising themselves. It's no wonder we are a pharmacological society, seeking the right drugs to make it all palatable. We are not living the life we were meant to live. Where is the joy in everyday life? How can you enjoy the sunset if you are so tired and busy you don't even realize what time it is. It is time to stop the insanity and get ready for the new awakening that is in progress.

There is a line being drawn in the sand and you will have to decide what you want, how you want to live and what is really important. The enemy is using your ego to lie to you; using your emotions and instincts to manipulate you. You are not what you feel, you are not what you own; you are a creation of God and you are predestined to achieve a purpose.

It is my responsibility to keep bringing this subject to the forefront of your mind because God has called me to attempt to wake the dead in faith and to help them seek the light. Stop, stop, stop letting the world keep you captive. It is making you a bird trapped in a gilded cage, keeping you distracted, and causing you to live in anxiety and fear. Fear keeps you separated from faith, and without faith you cannot live in the light of God and walk in His guidance. Residing within you are the powers and the faith of Lord and you can rebuke your fears and walk in peace.

> **Matthew 8:25.** *And the disciples came to the Lord and said," Lord save us, we perish. And the Lord said unto them Why are you fearful, Oh you of little*

A New Age of God

faith?" Then He arose and rebuked the winds and the sea; and there was a great calm.

God can rebuke the storm in your life and can bring you peace and calm. There is a quickening occurring in our time; information is bombarding us at faster and faster rates, technology and research keeps doubling what we can do. The world seems to think technology is the answer to everything. There is also an awakening of the spirit that is occurring in God's children too. We are being urged to listen to the voice within, to pay attention to the inner being and start the awakening that God wants us to heed. The quickening of the Spirit is working with certain people sending visions and dreams. There is an urging like a feeling there is something you need to do but you can't remember what it is.

There is a Spiritual mandate for these people to unite to prepare for the tremendous changes that are happening right now... We are at cross-roads on this planet. False leaders are surfacing that will tell us anything to get into power and there is a group of very powerful people who are working in the background behind the corporations and elections to manipulate all phases of government. They are seek to use religion and fear to change the landscape of the world. They want upheaval of every government and the collapse of the dollar so we can unite under one currency and one government so there can be equal control on all fronts.

It will sound good to all those fearful people who just want the government to take care of them. Their aim is to bring us to a one world government and force us to homogenize our beliefs or to completely walk away from our faith. They will instigate religious wars to prove religion is dangerous and should be eliminated. They believe we are all walking around asleep, and have no

A New Age of God

idea what is happening in the world. To them we are just puppets being manipulated by pulling our strings; whatever they decide is our fate.

The revolutions in the Middle East are just the beginning of the upheaval that is going to spread upon the Earth. They are using the Book of Revelations as a guide to bring forth their vision of a better world. They are playing GOD to recreate the world in their image. The enemy is using these egotists to bring havoc into the world. Soon it will become illegal to go to church or gather for worship. Every 4 minutes someone is martyred for their faith in Christ. In some countries of Africa if you are a Christian you will be tortured to denounce your faith and if you won't you are either killed or sold into slavery.

Everything they do starts out for your own good! Every time the government gives you a protection they take one or more of your rights away. The congress of the United States is diminishing and nullifying the bill of rights. It is time to wake up and start to think for yourself because they will eventually come for you. I am ready to stand up and if necessary die for my rights and beliefs and I know I am not alone in this, but I am not ready to kill for any of them. I am not condoning terrorism, forming militias or any other radical cause. This war is to be fought on the spiritual plane and at the ballot box. We have not yet come to the point where physical violence will be necessary, that is a discussion for the end of days.

I know there are lots survivalists that are stocking up guns and ammo to put up their last stand against the new world order, but that is not the war I am talking about. This war is fought through faith in God and standing up in your spiritual armor and swinging your sword of faith against the oppressors that wield doubt and dissention to separate us. Their goal is to keep us

A New Age of God

judging each other in self-righteous indignation and keep the Christian faith destroying each other.

We must use our greatest weapon on the enemy and that is love. If we love each other despite our differences, we can defeat the enemy and change the world's perception of what it takes to be a follower of Christ. We are the only faith that worships a living God that resides within each and every one of us. Our God empowers us to create our own life, to experience healings and miracles and to know the joy and peace of forgiveness in our everyday life.

Every day of my life is a miracle and I would die before I would deny the God who loves and guides my every step. He is the power that fuels my very existence and without Him residing within me I would be dead anyway. There is a war going on right now and it is life and death. We are fighting for our spiritual lives and most people don't even see it. The world wants you to just exist and leave all that God stuff behind. Don't fall for the veil of deceit that has fallen upon the eyes of mankind. Do not allow yourself to be the walking dead; just going through the motions of your humdrum everyday life.

I was the walking dead before I allowed God to change my life and now I have the Holy Spirit dwelling within me, giving me the daily bread that feeds my life. He is the Holy God that forgives my short comings and inspires my life. He shows me where I err every day so I may have the Grace to see them in others, and forgive them for being as human as I am.

Every day I see people who have the kindest hearts and want to do the right thing but just cannot commit to God because they cannot believe in a God that would allow the things that happen every day to go on in this world. They have been taught hell fire and brimstone and a God of vengeance. They have been taught that God sits on a throne just looking for a reason to punish you, much like

A New Age of God

the Greeks believed their Gods did on mount Olympus. This is the result of the gnostic (logical) thinkers that reworked the bible to meet their concept of reasoning out how God thinks of us all.

We have to stand and overcome the animal within and become the human we were originally created to be. God gave us Jesus to teach us to live in spirit and to operate in the word. He gave us the way in the light, taught us that we live in death without the light of the Holy Spirit, and the path to eliminate the animal within. The only problem is that when Jesus walked the earth He was seen as a radical that threatened the church and even today His philosophy and original teachings has always threatened the elevated security self-proclaimed authority of the priesthood that kept the common man separated from God. His philosophy was so heretical that His original teachings were suppressed and changed to allow God to be perceived in the manner He had always been seen and worshipped.

When Jesus was placed on the cross the sky became as night, at the moment Jesus died on the cross the veil in the temple split in two pieces (which reopened the spiritual plane for man's access), when Jesus was taken down from the cross the moment His body touched the ground the earth shook as if an earthquake hit the temple. The sun did not shine again until Jesus had died. The people shook in fear because they knew the blood of an innocent had been spilled and feared the wrath of God for executing one so Holy. The priests knew what they had done and feared the people would rise up and kill them for killing the Messiah.

They begged the romans to place the guard and seal the tomb so the body could not be stolen so the prophecy of the resurrection could be faked. They wanted to prove they had not killed the Messiah and all they did was

A New Age of God

confirm the fact that He had truly risen. All their efforts did was to prove to the people a miracle had occurred and the Messiah had risen. Jesus told them if they tore down the temple (His body) He would rebuild it in three days. On the third day the Messiah rose, cast off His bindings and walked out of the cave.

Jesus walked the earth for 40 days after the crucifixion teaching and leading the people. The mystery is what did Jesus teach in those 40 days? He gave the world His abilities through the Holy Spirit so that we could do the works of God ourselves. I believe God is working through those He is calling us through the people He is giving visions and through those He is inspiring to make an attempt to put into human words what He is explaining to us through His guidance.

The people today operate under the misconception that God unilaterally will come down and smote the evildoers of this world. They don't understand if there is a God then why does He allows all this evil to run rampant in the world. That is the greatest misunderstanding there is. God empowered us with free will and dominion on the Earth. We have all the power Jesus had when He walked the land and through Jesus we have the ability to create our lives, but unfortunately that is a double edged sword and man can use that power for evil as well. That is why Satan wants to seduce us into misusing that power and allow the enemy to wreak havoc in our lives through our own minds and words.

As stated earlier, God gave man dominion on the Earth and we have to clean up our own mess. We can no longer allow evil to run rampant in our neighborhoods. We can't leave it up to the other guy to fix, we have to stand up and not tolerate the evil of drugs and alcohol to ruin our lives. Every drug purchased not only destroys the user

A New Age of God

but impacts his neighborhood and empowers the drug lords to destroy everything they touch.

The violence of the drug cartels are destroying Mexico and other third world countries and they will do the same here if our police and our government could be purchased as easily as it has been done there. Every day they infiltrate our lands and bring their poison and violence to our front doors. The people continue to crave the drugs and finance the terrorism we are trying to stop. We cannot expect the police to control what we are allowing to run rampant through our communities. It is not just the poor and the ignorant that is being harmed, it is our future that is being destroyed along with our children.

We must take up our spiritual armor and pick up our sword of justice and stand up for our rights and make this a better world before we lose it completely, because if we don't and Jesus returns with the sunrise, we will have to answer to Him and explain why we sat idly by waiting for someone else to take care of it. The longer Jesus tarries the longer we have to do His work and create a better world.

We have allowed the animal filled child molesters to infiltrate the churches and neighborhoods. Human trafficking still goes on every day; our children do not get a chance to be innocent because we have allowed sex, drugs and pornography to infiltrate the music, the movies and every day on the television in their living room. They can't play outside anymore for fear that someone will abduct them. For many perverted souls sex is their only religion and they do not see innocence or purity, they only see an object for their personal use. This is an animal insanity of Satan and it must be wiped from the Earth. This is a disease of pandemic proportions and it must be stopped.

How can you deny it, evil is running rampant and we have made it glamorous and attractive. I am not crying

A New Age of God

wolf, because the wolf is already at the door ready to pounce if you leave the door open.

God is calling us to do his works. We are seeing visions and having premonitions. Once upon a time it was the job of men to lead prophesize and teach, but that time has passed because the men have lost their way and God knows our hearts are open to His love and guidance. We are being called to change or way of thinking and living so we can change the world.

It is time for all of us to answer the call and understand this is the ultimate teacher calling you to His school, to teach you how to live in His light and follow His guidance. He wants you to heal the wounds man has inflicted upon itself through hatred, intolerance and differences of the religions of man. He is the light of the world and he will light the way if you allow Him into your life and into your heart.

If we let the true light of the world lead us we will eliminate prejudice, religious persecution and distrust from our hearts and see the truth we can change the world and make it as it was created to be.

I have been told I am a dreamer and an idealist and maybe I am, but my dreams and ideals come from my sweet Lord who guides my mind and my life. I am trying to fulfill His will in all I do and I want to move you to accept this challenge and bring to your life the guiding touch of the Holy Spirit.

If I touch just one person and help bring them closer to God then I am a success. If I touch a nerve in the consciousness of man and help start a revolution then I am honored beyond words. I feel I must tell you that all I do and all I write is inspired by God and some of it is dictated by the Holy Spirit to help the lost find their way home. The Father of us all loves you beyond words and thought and He wants you to know there is a way home to Him. He resides within the hearts and minds of those who seek. He is the Holy of Holies who loves you as if you are His only child.

You are His precious gift to the world and all that has passed before today is like the waves in the water, they cause a wake of disturbance and then they dissipate. The only way they go on is if you continue to disturb the water. Let Him take the weight of the past away and allow Him to say peace be still to the waters of your mind. Allow Jesus to give you the peace of salvation and gain the favor of the Lord.

There is no pain He cannot heal, no hurt he cannot ease and all you have to do is lay it at the foot of His cross and give it to Him. He suffered the stripes from the whip to take your pain; the blood that ran to the ground was the Holy blood of the Father, and He suffered the sacrifice on the cross for you so you could have salvation and receive the Holy Spirit into your life. He chose to suffer for you and take the pain of the sins of the world so you could seek salvation and live the life you were intended to live. What are you willing to do to repay His sacrifice?

All you have to do is believe in the divinity of Jesus Christ; that He died on the Cross for you, that He is resurrected and lives to this day. One little whisper to Him in faith is all it takes to change your life forever and receive the gift that He has been waiting to bestow upon you.

Visions and Prophecy

The awakening of the Spirit is causing more people to experience visions and have prophetic experiences such as those that come in dreams. The logical mind

A New Age of God

cannot understand the working in visions, that is the realm of faith. When you experience visions you are getting a peek at the eternal realm. If you try to decipher and understand what and why, you will be frustrated and confused. Only through the Holy Spirit can you understand and interpret.

In the bible prophecies may skip around between thousands of years. The Old Testament is full of prophecy for the coming of the Messiah and the New Testament is the fulfillment, proclamation and explanation of the Messiah.

Think about God's timeline compared to our Earthly time frame. God created the heaven and the Earth in one day, now think about how long it took for the universe to form according to scientists.

God has been communicating and directing His people throughout the ages. Since the time of Abraham when God sent a priest named Melchizedek to Abraham. (Hebrews 7:3) Melchizedek had no Mother, or Father or genealogy; without beginning of days or without end. He inspired and guided Abraham then departed and was never seen again. Some believe He was the Messiah coming to lead Abraham on the correct path and then he returned to the Father.

I don't agree that Melchizedek was the Messiah but there is a Messianic spirit that inspires certain people through the generations to attempt to move the people to unite under the one God and work together. It is possible to do the work of and for the Messiah and not be Him, but be guided by Him to give His guidance and His word to the world.

You too can achieve this level of spirituality with work and devotion. It has to be a selfless task and it has to be the dominating purpose of your life to serve God. You

A New Age of God

don't have to be a priest or a minister just love God and want to serve.

I have been seeing visions and have prophetic dreams all my life. The more I pray the higher level I achieve reaching for the Lord, the more I meditate the clearer my visions. There are visions and dreams that are not sent in the name of God, they are sent to mislead you and aim to keep you distracted because do not want you to achieve your purpose just be careful how you interpret what how you receive. The more they work to deter your progress the more frightened they are of your work; the greater the attack the greater your reward. You must be very careful and learn to discern who and what is of God. You must ask if they believe that Jesus died on the cross to bring salvation and the Holy Spirit to the world. Ask if this guidance is sent in the name of Jesus to fulfill the works of God. If they are not of God they will depart or will answer no. Regardless of who they are or who sent them they cannot swear to be of God if they are not.

We must be cautious of where we get out inspiration and guidance. We all have guides, guardians and teachers that work to help us in all we do to grow closer to the Father and to do His work. We must always pray for the protection of Jesus and request only the guidance through the Holy Spirit.

Some people are heavily influenced by the Jezebel spirit. Jezebel strives to cause strife and separation in the church. She leads people especially women to be self-righteous, willful and judgmental and has taken down many a church. We all should work to keep her influence from separating the people in your congregation. If you know someone who is always criticizing the pastor and gossiping about others in the church especially if they point out how holy someone thinks they are, then you have a jezebel spirit working against your pastor and your

A New Age of God

church. Jezebel loves to take a point of law in the church and start to cause division making a point to show the differences in belief.

There are no perfect churches, just as there are no perfect people. The secret is to keep your eyes and ears on God and do not allow any distractions. There is always someone or something trying to plant seeds of deceit in your life. Seeds of deceit are the little lies that take root within the spirit and become major obstacles once they take root and grow. We all have them from our childhood or from things we have read or heard. They can be recognized as prejudice, bigotry, superiority or any number of dirty little things that seep into our minds and seem harmless. We must love each other and allow others to find their way.

I know it is a difficult time to try to discern what prejudice is and what is justified when there is so much evil and hatred in the world. Islam hates the Christians and the Jews and the Americans hate Islam because of the Twin Towers. The war rages on in Iraq and Afghanistan year after year. As of this writing Guantanamo has been holding prisoners for 10 years and if they weren't terrorists before they are now. Where will it end? How do we stop the spiral of hate and distrust between two major factions of the world?

Only through God can we find a healing for our hearts and the world. God wants us to work together to mend our hearts and our minds. Only through love can we truly heal. I am not saying tolerating evil is the solution but the gun only begets more guns. Hate inspires hate. Love can inspire love and the righteousness of God can solve our problems.

God is calling you home! It is up to you to answer the call. Many are chosen but few accept the call. We must begin to be bold in our faith and show our love. We must unite

A New Age of God

in faith and work together or God will forsake us unto our own creation and we will fall to the enemy. There is a tremendous call being made by God for a revival of the spirit. There is going to be that revival and millions of people are going to answer the call and begin to work together to heal our lives, our families and our countries.

Every country is being called to awaken, recognize and understand the truth and stop believing the lies that have torn us apart for so long. Let's all try a little prayer, a little praise of the Father and a little understanding and see if we can build a better society.

A message from the Holy Spirit for the book:

The love of God must be shown. The love of our Father is endless and you must be a church for His love. To the people, God sends His love. The Father of us all is distressed that His children are not devoted to the Lord. The Father of us all wants us to see a rebirth of awareness of His love and of the love you are to show each other.

The works of the Father of us all is to compose a brotherhood of the faithful before it is all lost to the Deceiver of mankind. The Father of us all is grieved that the professors of faith have let doubt stop the works of God.

The Father of us all needs mankind to begin to prepare for the great upheaval to come. You need to be ready for war. The Father of us all is not going to stand for a people that do not honor Him. The love of God will not be assimilated into Pagan beliefs. The Father of us all is THE ONLY GOD and there are so few on the clock for God.

The love of one woman is the reason we are telling the world. The love of God has moved the Father of us all to tell the woman his heart and to inspire a book on what it means to worship and how to reach out to the Lord. The love of one woman was enough to bring the Father of us all into words.

Men of God take heed you are living in the midst of the next great awakening of Spirit. The Father of us all is the light and the way and you need to choose to awaken. Watch what you watch; words are the tool to how you live. The word is God and the fall of the people is all in the word.

One life eternal...One love unending...One God....

CHAPTER 10

A Final Explanation

My precious Father is calling you to wake up and realize what is going on in the world and for us to join into a brotherhood of His righteousness and come to the defense of the word. We have been lied to and misled; we have been hypnotized by the great Deceiver to live within our own egos and needs. We have allowed evil to rule mankind long enough. It is time to make a stand and learn how to live a true life in God's light. Join me in making a stand for the love and unity of mankind, free from the animal that rules within.

The Pagan influence God was speaking of revolves around the changes made in the Church by Constantine 1. Constantine a Roman by birth was a pagan and worshipped the sun god until he decided to become a Christian. Before his so called conversion he persecuted the Jews and the Christians mercilessly. He held forth a council of Bishops of the church to unify the doctrine of Christianity. Once they had decided on what Christianity was to be they persecuted and killed everyone they could find who refused to follow their doctrine. Any conflicting materials were either destroyed or hidden.

A New Age of God

When Constantine reformed the church he performed an abomination unto the Father. He took his pagan beliefs of gods and along with the influences of the pagan church in Egypt (both heavily influenced by the sun god) and merged the beliefs into Christianity. In the Council of Nicaea the decree went out for the Christian Church to begin to celebrate Easter. They were told to observe the customs of the Romans and of Egypt who have celebrated Easter <u>since ancient times.</u>

> **Acts 12:4.** *And when he had apprehended him (Peter) he put him in prison. And delivered him to four quaternions of soldiers to keep him; intending after Easter to bring him before the people.*

The people who were persecuting Apostles were celebrating Easter? Wait a minute Easter is supposed to honor the resurrection of Christ but these people were not Christians, this was a pagan holiday. Easter was not initiated to observe the resurrection of Christ but it was the pagan holiday of fertility. The rabbit and the egg both are symbols of fertility in the pagan beliefs. For approximately 1,950 years the Christian people have been told a lie and have been celebrating a pagan holiday under the guise of honoring Christ's resurrection. The date was chosen for spring solstice (a pagan time of ritual) not for when they thought Jesus rose from the dead.

Christmas was selected to coincide with the winter solstice not for when Christ was born. The winter solstice was a vital part of pagan tradition and by putting Christ's name on the ritual times they were able to get the pagans to accept Christianity.

The fact that we celebrate Halloween is a tribute to witchcraft. I understand that it is only done in fun

A New Age of God

and only an excuse to dress up but to God it we are celebrating evil. It might be make believe but the subconscious mind just believes and it opens up the door for other influences to begin to make their way into the mind.

God gave mankind paradise but we weren't satisfied with walking with God. We had to defy Him and wound up drawing the veil between us to live in separation. God sent the Son to show us the way out of religion and give us the Kingdom. He suffered the cross to eliminate the veil and allow us direct intercession with God through the Holy Spirit. Christ paid the ultimate price for you.

God has reached out to His children time after time and mankind has had to ruin each opportunity. God is tired of our disobedience and blindness.

When God provided me with this revelation I became very angry. I felt betrayed by a religion that professed to be for God and was supposedly there to guide me to God. I was angry at mankind for turning its back of God and for altering the teachings of Jesus. I cried out to God and begged for forgiveness for mankind's stupidity and for allowing our so called logic to change one thing that was divinely sent to save us. Jesus came to give us the Kingdom within through His teachings. His principals are the ONLY thing we are supposed to honor and worship. If it is not of God leave it alone and get away from it.

How can God honor His children that pay homage and honor to pagan holidays and rituals? This is not a small thing to God and He will not suffer our disobedience. He will withdraw His favor and we will live once again in separation until we atone and get back to a Godly life. We wonder why God does not honor us with His presence in our lives and do not understand why we are lost to God. We raise our hands to God and ask why we feel so lost.

A New Age of God

We are lost because we have been taught lies that we have accepted as truths that offend the Father.

God is calling us to purify our faith. Seek out all the pagan lies and eliminate them from our worship. Use the power of the Holy Spirit to subdue the carnal mind and put the animal to rest. Honor the One God, the Father of us all. We must clear all the abominations against God in our celebrations, our worship and our lives.

We have become a people without honor. We have strived to have separation of church and state and a house divided cannot stand. A world without honor cannot survive. We need to look at our faith, our countries and our lives from God's perspective and imagine how God sees us.

We flock to movies that glorify hate and evil. Our major celebrations involve centuries old pagan rituals. We have taken something that is supposed to be pure and a gift of love; a spiritual experience and have turned it into sex: the recreational sport.

We spend thousands of dollars on a big church wedding, take sacred vow and within 3 years we get a divorce. Things get difficult and we cut and run. The status quo is to live together, maybe have a few children and then maybe you'll decide to get married. What the heck the kids will enjoy the wedding too!

Meanwhile our kids are being raised by strangers and watching movies that promote witchcraft or God only knows what else. God doesn't get a word mentioned unless it is to make Him look inferior to the evil one, but you sure hear a lot of the other stuff. I am begging you to take a good look at the world for what it has really become. Witness it for yourself. Do your own research into the history of the church and decide for yourself. I don't want to tell you what to believe, I just want you to

A New Age of God

start questioning what is going on and start thinking for yourself.

True men of God recognize the truth when they see it. They may not like it but they recognize it. Get angry for what they took from you and reclaim your inheritance as a child of the Most High God. You are a child of royal blood and they have tried for almost 2,000 years to keep you from your inheritance. The secret to life is to love God, honor Him in all you do, give Him the glory and to love your neighbor as you love yourself.

God is calling His children home. He wants you to live an abundant life in joy. Give yourself the chance to be happy and live in the peace and serenity of the Father. He came to us in the form of Jesus and He speaks to us in the form of the Holy Spirit. They are three but they are one spirit.

There are going to be many religious leaders who will hate what I have written here. They will try to discredit my words and attempt to keep you trapped in dogma. The enemy is going to fight this message with all his might. We are getting ready to witness many miracles and wonders in the world and many so called prophets will arise.

Our job is to keep our eyes and hearts open to Devine guidance to recognize the truth. Do they operate in the name of Jesus? Do they honor the Father and give Him the glory for what they do? Are they operating under the anointing of the Holy Spirit?

Many miracles will be performed in other names, the occult will be used to manifest what appears to be of God but it will not be of God. Be aware of those things that want to lead you away from the Father and use your inner spirit to guide your heart. All that shines is not gold and not all who seek your worship are not of God.

A New Age of God

The Father demands you to worship only Him without false idols or intercessors. Jesus said to seek the Father through the Son and the Father will hear you. False idols and false religious practices have infiltrated the church and they must be cleansed for us to truly honor the Father. It is time to stop living by tradition but to wake up and start asking questions and seek the truth for you.

> *To be a leader you must be bold...To be a teacher you must lead... To be a student you must submit... To be a Christian you must love....One life...One love...eternal.*

I wish you the peace of the Father of us all in your quest for the truth.

www.ingramcontent.com/pod-product-compliance
Lightning Source LLC
Chambersburg PA
CBHW031640040426
42453CB00006B/167